The Prodigal Daughter & Her Dad

Conversations back-and-forth
about life's challenges with
bible verses and worship songs

By Bola and Andrea Ogunkoya

I dedicate this book to God Almighty
who by His grace has preserved
my life.

To my wife Niyi and my children who
have been my pillars of support.

Bola

For my Jack & India.
Every breath has been for you.

..and of course my Dad, the
epitome of unconditional love.

Andrea

Contents

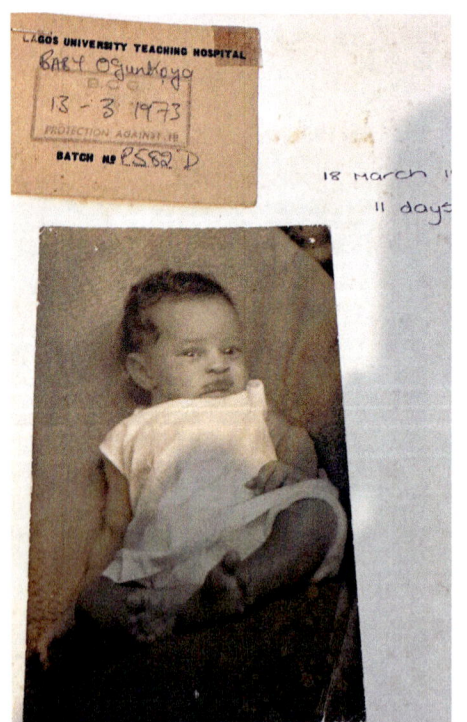

INTRODUCTION

50 Questions and answers about everyday life.

After four decades of ups, downs and almost every family crisis you can think of including divorce, drugs, prison, homelessness, domestic violence, poverty, death, betrayal, suicide, infidelity and more we are writing this book in the hope that the lessons we have learned, quite often the hard way, and the way we have supported each other will help others.

We have definitely not always agreed but we have always had open communication. **If your life and relationships are imperfect this is for you.** We ask difficult questions and debate the narrative. We are not experts, just two people, a Dad and his Daughter that have been through lots and now share our journey, with real excerpts of what we said to each other in the moment with some of what has worked for us, with you.

Our foundation has been our faith. We express and practise our Christianity differently. Go to different kinds of churches and debate biblical interpretations. None the less this has been our cornerstone that has through everything always brought us back together and allowed the love to prevail.

I have often asked my Dad questions and his answers have both comforted and surprised me. If you are anything like me it's great to have someone who does not just tell you what you want or expect to hear.

We are very aware that not everyone has a good relationship with their earthly father. For those who don't have a Dad that they can or want to turn to and ask, I share my Dad and his (almost) 80 years of wisdom which always has God at its centre, with you.

A note about reading the book.

There are 50 questions and answers. Some will appeal to you more than others. Some may be exactly what you need to ask and read about right now based on what is going on in your life while others may be something you turn to another time. Please don't feel that you have to start at the beginning and read every page till the last. We are often guided by what we need with exactly the right stepping stone at just the right time. So, turn to the pages that speak to you.

Andrea was writing this from England with Bola in Nigeria so much of the book was written over WhatsApp chats. In places we have thought it appropriate to simply share the exact text as it was typed in the moment. Bola prefers the Kings James Bible while Andrea prefers the New International Version (NIV), so we have included passages with both!

About Bola & Andrea

Bola was born Bolanle Ogunkoya to Mr Abel and Mrs Adeola Ogunkoya at Ibadan, Western Nigeria (now Oyo State) on 3rd January 1945.

He attended St. James' Primary School, Oke-Ado in Ibadan for six years, then Ibadan Boys High School from 1959-1963. He worked as a Produce Examiner at the Old Western Nigeria Ministry of Agriculture from 1963 - 1965. This took him around most of the Old Western Region of Owo, Akure, Ondo, Emure, Ise-Ekiyi, grading coco and palm kernels which he had received adequate training for.

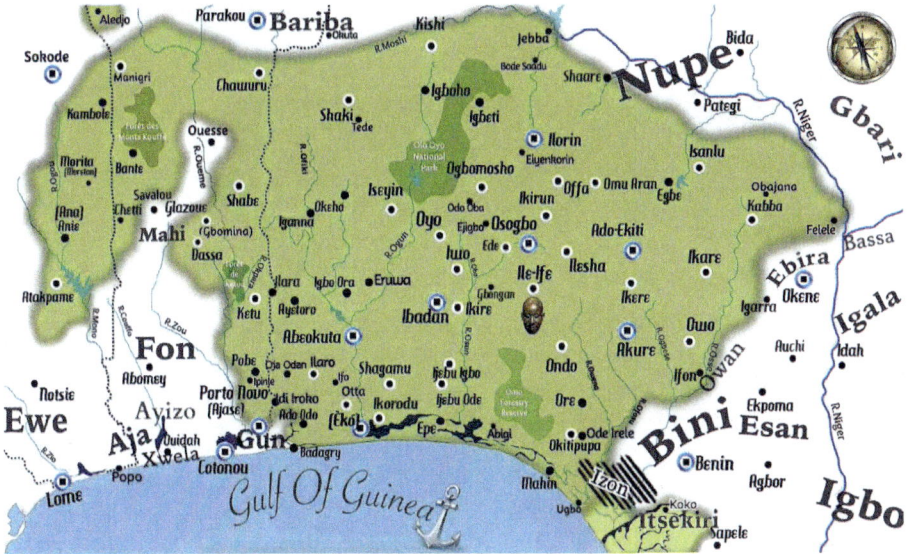

Map by Oramfe - Own work, CC BY-SA 4.0

Bola saved up money and moved to Blackburn in Lancashire, England in 1965. He had two jobs including one on a farm where one of the perks was getting to take home a chicken. He remembers he always ate well. He drove a navy blue Triumph Spitfire and unbelievably still remembers the licence plate: ETE536B.

He graduated in textiles Technology at the Blackburn College in 1970 and got a job back home with Afprint (Nig) LTD Lagos in 1971 as a textiles technologist. He had an early promotion but left in 1975 to join P.Z (Nig) LTD as Textiles Sales Manager, Lagos. In 1973 (the year his first child Andrea was born) he was transferred to head the department of textiles in Kano, Northern Nigeria.

In 1975 he was recalled to Lagos to proceed to London and attend the Industrial Society to read Personnel Management and Industrial Relations. He returned home to become Personnel Manager of P.Z. (Nigeria) LTD till 1980.

He left P.Z (Nig) LTD to join SCOA (Nig) LTD as Regional Manager Textiles North. By the end of 1981 he had left the corporate world to start his own business called LeChem Nig LTD as a general importer and electronics wholesale and retail outfit.

Along the way he has also owned a medium sized poultry farm, tennis supply shop and Internet cafe. He was also into sachet water manufacturing.

He is an Associate Member of the British Institute of Management (1978), affiliate member of the Nigerian Institute of Personnel Management, Bola held a post graduate diploma in Business Management and an MBA.

Bola had a passion for tennis playing and involved in many administrative roles. He was a Veteran Tennis Champion (Nigeria) in 1991 and was the

Secretary of the Organising Committee of the famous Dala Hard Court Tennis Championships from 1989 to 2005 when he was promoted to Tournament Director.

With a reputation as a very hardworking and diligent man, always concerned about legality.

An Elder of the Redeemed Christian Church of God, he commanded the respect of all his friends and spiritual leaders. In 1991 he took time off to attend bible school of discipleship and had also been significantly involved in church activities. An Elder of the Redeemed Christian Church of God, he commands the respect of all his friends and spiritual leaders. 2014-2015 Bola got a Post Graduate Diploma (distinction) in Theology from The Redeemed Bible College.

When asked how he wanted to be remembered Bola said, "A good Father and husband who loved his family with the love of God. Kind and compassionate, who will be remembered for his ministry of reconciliation man to man and man up God, kindness and the pursuance of peace".

Bola's Children
Andrea Yetunde
Sonia Adetola
Biodun
Bimbo
Laide
Feyi

About Yoruba History

The Yoruba people are a West African ethnic group who mainly inhabit parts of Nigeria, Benin, and Togo. The areas of these countries primarily inhabited by the Yoruba are often collectively referred to as Yorubaland. The Yoruba constitute more than 52 million people in Africa, are over a million outside the continent, and bear further representation among members of the African diaspora. The vast majority of the Yoruba population is today within the Nigeria, where they make up 21% of the country's population making them one of the largest ethnic groups in Africa. Most Yoruba people speak the Yoruba language, which is the Niger-Congo language with the largest number of native speakers.

Based on oral and written sources, this name existed before the 1500s. The oldest known textual reference to the name Yoruba is found in an essay (titled – Mi'rāj al-Su'ūd) from a manuscript written by the Berber jurist Ahmed Baba in 1614.

By the 8th century, a powerful kingdom already existed in Ile-Ife, one of the earliest in Africa. It is said to be Ile-gbo (capital of the realm of humanity, based on the oldest pre-dynastic traditions of its being associated with Oba Tala, Oro-gbo (Sango) and Otete (Oduduwa).

Some Yoruba cities of the Middle Ages

Oral history recorded under the Oyo Empire derives the Yoruba as an ethnic group from the population of the older kingdom of Ile-Ife. The Yoruba were the dominant cultural force in southern and Northern, Eastern Nigeria as far back as the 11th century.

The Yoruba are among the most urbanized people in Africa. For centuries before the arrival of the British colonial administration most Yoruba already lived in well structured urban centres organized around powerful city-states centred around the residence of the Oba (king). In ancient times, most of these cities were fortresses, with high walls and gates.Yoruba cities have always been among the most populous in Africa. Archaeological findings indicate that Òyó-Ilé or Katunga, capital of the Yoruba empire of Oyo had a population of over 100,000 people. For a long time also, Ibadan, one of the major Yoruba cities and founded in the 1800s, was the largest city in the whole of Sub Saharan Africa. Today, Lagos (Yoruba: Èkó), another major Yoruba city, with a population of over twenty million, remains the largest on the African continent.

About Andrea

I was born in Lagos Nigeria in the affluent West Africa of 1973. My childhood years were spent in the northern city of Kano that borders the Sahara desert and then had a 90% Muslim/10% Christian population. As a result my childhood was extremely diverse with a big expat community and friends spanning myriad countries and faiths.

We were members of the private tennis club "Kano Club" and I spent endless days there swimming, watching the tennis, on the playground with friends and eating lunch in the restaurant after church. My Dad was a heavyweight boxing fan and I have memories sitting with him watching boxing or tennis both (well mostly him!) yelling at the screen.

"Haba! This man is behind-o and he is chopping banana! Better stand up and get serious"

Growing up I went to school in England and spent most summers with my Dad and loved it! I always felt like I fit in better and belonged when I was there. It was always an adventure with loads of parties that I was not allowed to go to. There was often a campaign enrolling everyone I could to try and convince my Dad. He always gave in to some, but was thoughtful about who I associated with, where I went and possible dangers. We were always close and I missed him terribly when I wasn't with him.

Today I have had a career in sales and marketing, I have lived in different countries and am a single mum to two amazing high achiever teenagers, both brought up as Christians and developing their own personal relationship with God. Although we all still love tennis and try and try to attend Wimbledon each year none of us became tennis players. However both my children are high level national swimmers. My Dad's involvement in competitive sport gave me an understanding of and appetite for the huge commitment. We regularly discuss swimming rankings, strategies, sportsmanship and results. My Dad lives in Ibadan and I live in England so we have lots of communication over WhatApp. He is usually the first text I get in the morning and the last message I send at night.

We have a special bond. I can't explain it. Even in these later years he once commented that other people did not want him to talk about death and he was glad he could talk to me about it. I have never been afraid of him dying. It doesn't seem morbid but somehow natural that we can talk to each other about all aspects of life and death is a part of that.

For me this is the greatest love story. We hope you enjoy it.

[04/01/2023, 5:22:59 am] Dad:

Good morning daughter.

I am sincerely proud of you as a child of a 78 year old man.

I am proud and happily delighted to be your Father.

I thank God for making us what we are.

I am eternally grateful for all you have done for me. The love and care, concern and compassion, prayers and generosity, accommodation, and patience.

God bless and reward you.

Love you.

[04/01/2023, 6:07:55 am] Andrea:

What a wonderful message for me to wake up to. What a gift those words are. They will stay with me forever. I am your prodigal daughter and you have always acted like the father does in the bible. Unconditional love. To know that you are loved, to know that someone thinks you're great … makes you manifest that and become great. For someone to be proud of you in spite of your failures allows you to forgive yourself and carry on. I only have one Dad and I wouldn't swap you for anyone. I am grateful for your consistent and unwavering love that has been there my whole 50 years. I have loved and been loved by you the longest. There is no one else that I have loved and has loved me for 50 years except you.

[04/01/2023, 6:36:55 am] Dad:

Tears of joy!

Question 1

Bola: As you grew up what did the word Father mean to you? What does it connote now over four decades? What a starting point!

[24/01/2023, 6:21:37 am] Andrea:

Good morning!

I love this and I just heard something on the radio the other day that Abba translated means more than father. There is an intimacy to it. It's closer in translation to Daddy. Some people when they think of "father" have good memories or thoughts. Others have bad associations of cruelty, hurt, disappointment or abuse.

For me despite the ups and downs of being a child of divorce, money problems and living for most of my life 4,000 miles apart here's what I always knew:

1. That you loved me. You told me often. You showed me with what you could when you could including phone calls in the days when they were terribly expensive and it would take us sometimes hours to get through on a very bad connection.

2. I was wanted. When you could afford the trip to England it was to see us. You bought me my first record album in Shepherds Bush, NWA.

3. You were interested in me, cared and had an opinion on the way I behaved and what I achieved.

4. Faith. You taught me the Lords Prayer and Psalm 23 when I was little. You prayed and made church an instrumental part of my early childhood. You talked about God like he was a close relative or friend. Familiar and comforting. You reminded me to pray, read my bible and go to church which I did with my Grandma who was the only one in the family that went. So we went together. When I was about 11 I signed myself up for my confirmation. I walked in the dark alone to the classes and talked and learned about God in more personal way. That you introduced me to my faith and encouraged me to keep going and keep connected to the community of a church family was unequivocally the best gift of my life.

5. You say you are sorry. You are not perfect and there have been mistakes and things that have hurt me. I have hurt you. You have always said you are sorry. Perhaps not in the exact moment of a heated argument and upset but you ponder it, reflect on it and then apologise. "I am terribly sorry that I hurt you". Full sincerity and humility. What does this do? Well …. it's impossible for me to stay mad at you when you do that! Whatever the situation it immediately defuses it. While there may be discussions still to be had and compromises to be made you calm things down by showing such care and compassion for how I feel. You do not tend to make excuses or say "sorry but…" you just lead the reconciliation with those powerful and impactful words that acknowledge my feelings.

There is so much this does in the moment but also it has shaped me as a person and particularly as a parent. It shows that it is ok to get it wrong even when you are the parent. I don't think you always believed you were wrong or most wrong every time you apologised but you said it for me. Out of love and because you figured out long before I did that ultimately it just wasn't worth it to have a standoff of who was right and who was wrong. You showed me grace.

So today as a mum to two gorgeous and highly opinionated teenagers I say I'm sorry. I pull them close at the exact moment I feel like pulling my hair out. I keep a personal relationship with God a part of our lives.

6. Consistency. You have definitely evolved and softened over the years but for the most part nothing has changed. Your moral compass solidly points north. You have had numerous opportunities for fraud and corruption that would have made you wealthy. You always turned them down. I think one of your key values is commitment. Once you are committed to something that's it. You we're committed to tennis and were a great player but also a friend to do many others. You had compassion for the shoeless ball boys and gave them all sorts. You gave your time on the committee and managing competitive events like Dala Championships. Although you have held several high end managerial positions for international companies you you are also an entrepreneur. Always looking for an opportunity to make a good living. Always keeping going and hustling through tough times.

Your consistency is a comfort. You are not a volatile person. I always know what to expect. This makes me feel safe.

So growing up the word father only meant you. Today when I think about the word father I think of my Heavenly Father and I think of you. People become fathers but I think you have earned the title and wear it proudly (or you should!) as a badge of honour. I think you know the responsibility that comes with being a father and that you have especially as you have got older mirrored your approach to fatherhood on God the Father regularly asking yourself "what would He do"?

For me I truly think that I am one of the lucky ones. When I think of "Father" today I have two and both have always been there for me, shown me love, mercy, compassion and consistency. Both are great.

As we both approach this new season of our lives with me almost 50 and you almost 80 whether we are here together on earth or not I will always think "what would my Dad do". Like the original translation of Abba you are my Daddy which is much more intimate a relationship than Father. We have a closeness and connection that has lasted the whole 4 decades and will transcend this world.

[24/01/2023, 6:40:54 am] Dad:

Just overwhelming and unbelievable and a God inspired piece.

[24/01/2023, 6:47:16 am] Andrea:

You should answer the same question you asked me too.

By the way you are in charge of adding in the biblical references. So for each question and answer please think about what verses we can add.

When someone asks what you are doing today you can now say "I'm writing a book with my eldest daughter"!

Love you!

[24/01/2023, 6:51:41 am] Dad:

What a marvellous task for a retired, struggling but contented elderly father!

 Malachi 1:6

21st Century King James Version

6 "A son honoreth his father, and a servant his master. If then I be a father, where is Mine honor? And if I be a master, where is the fear of Me? saith the Lord of hosts unto you, O priests, who despise My name. And ye say, 'Wherein have we despised Thy name?'

Malachi 1:6

New International Version
Breaking Covenant Through Blemished Sacrifices

6 "A son honours his father, and a slave his master. If I am a father, where is the honour due me? If I am a master, where is the respect due me?" says the Lord Almighty.

"It is you priests who show contempt for my name.

"But you ask, 'How have we shown contempt for your name?'

Worship Song
Recommendation

The Blessing

Lyrics:

The Lord bless you

And keep you

Make His face shine upon you

And be gracious to you

The Lord turn His

Face toward you

And give you peace

Amen, amen, amen

Amen, amen, amen

The Lord bless you

And keep you

Make His face shine upon you

And be gracious to you

The Lord turn His

Face toward you

And give you peace

Amen, amen, amen (we sing, we sing)

Amen, amen, amen

May His favor be upon you

And a thousand generations

And your family and your children

And their children, and their children

May His favor be upon you

And a thousand generations

And your family and your children

And their children, and their children

May His presence go before you

And behind you, and beside you

All around you, and within you

He is with you, He is with you

In the morning, in the evening

In your coming, and your going

In your weeping, and rejoicing

He is for you, He is for you

He is for you, He is for you

He is for you, He is for you

He is for you, He is for you (I know, I know)

Amen, amen, amen

Amen, amen, amen

May His presence go before you

And behind you, and beside you

All around you, and within you

He is with you, He is with you

In the morning, in the evening

In your coming, and your going

In your weeping, and rejoicing

He is for you

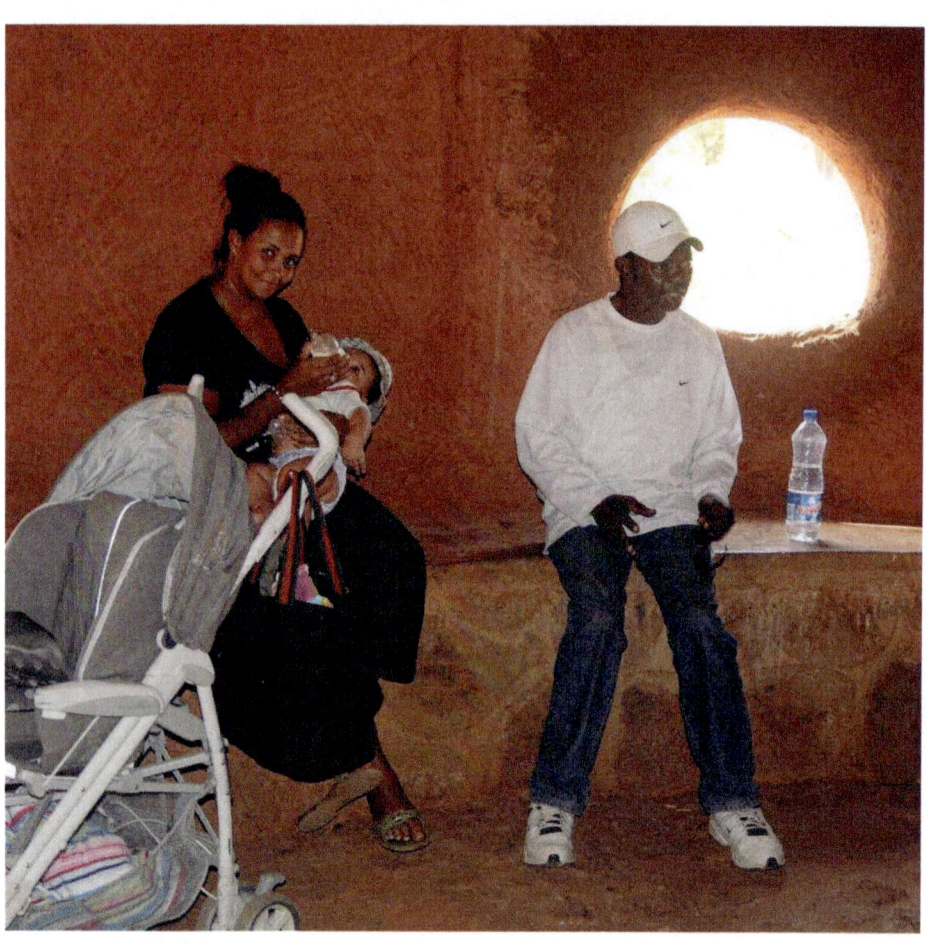

Question 2:

[29/01/2023, 5:21:13 am] Andrea:

Have you got anything new for our book today?

[29/01/2023, 5:26:29 am] Dad:

My adopted Name Yehosua.

Hebrew name for Joshua. My baptismal name is Joshua. Did you know?

At UCH I am announced as Joshua Bola Ogunkoya!

[29/01/2023, 7:53:40 am] Andrea:

I have heard of Joshua but did not know it was your baptism name.

[29/01/2023, 7:57:30 am] Andrea:

We don't give people new names here when they are baptised. **Do you think that people who are baptised can completely reinvent themselves? It makes me think about people who commit crimes like murder or rape and then go to prison say they have found the Lord and are a new person. What do you think about that? Is it possible or are people right to be sceptical?**

[29/01/2023, 7:57:59 am] Andrea:

If you're rushing for church just answer later or when you can. 🥰

[29/01/2023, 8:06:17 am] Dad:

Baptism is dying and rising with Christ. It depends on the state of the heart.

The Bible says that our love should be without dissimulation (deceit, pretence and hypocrisy)

Unless you are filled with the holy spirit and you operate in the His power it is a futile exercise.

Galatians 5 16 - Walk in the Spirit and you will not fulfil the lust of the flesh

21st Century King James Version

5 Stand fast therefore in the liberty wherewith Christ hath made us free, and be not entangled again with the yoke of bondage.

2 Behold, I, Paul, say unto you that if ye be circumcised, Christ shall profit you nothing.

3 For I testify again to every man who is circumcised, that he is a debtor to keep the whole law.

4 Christ then becomes of no effect unto you, whosoever of you claim justification by the law; ye are fallen from grace.

5 For we, through the Spirit, wait for the hope of righteousness by faith.

6 For in Jesus Christ neither circumcision availeth anything, nor uncircumcision, but faith which worketh by love.

7 Ye were running well; who hindered you, that ye should not obey the truth?

8 This persuasion cometh not from Him that calleth you.

9 A little leaven leaveneth the whole lump.

10 I have confidence in you through the Lord that ye will be not otherwise minded; but he that troubleth you shall bear his judgment, whosoever he be.

11 And I, brethren, if I yet preach circumcision, why then do I yet suffer persecution? Then would the offense of the cross cease.

12 I would that they were even cut off which trouble you!

13 For, brethren, ye have been called unto liberty; only use not liberty for an occasion of the flesh, but by love serve one another.

14 For all the law is fulfilled in one word, even in this: "Thou shalt love thy neighbor as thyself."

15 But if ye bite and devour one another, take heed that ye not be consumed one by another.

16 This I say then: Walk in the Spirit, and ye shall not fulfill the lust of the flesh.

17 For the flesh lusteth against the Spirit, and the Spirit against the flesh; and these are contrary the one to the other, so that ye cannot do the things that ye would.

18 But if ye are led by the Spirit, ye are not under the law.

19 Now the works of the flesh are manifest, and they are these: adultery, fornication, uncleanness, lasciviousness,

20 idolatry, witchcraft, hatred, quarreling, rivalry, wrath, strife, seditions, heresies,

21 envying, murders, drunkenness, revelings, and such like. About these things I tell you again, as I have also told you in times past, that those who do such things shall not inherit the Kingdom of God.

22 But the fruit of the Spirit is love, joy, peace, longsuffering, gentleness, goodness, faith,

23 meekness, temperance: against such there is no law.

24 And those who are Christ's have crucified the flesh with its affections and lusts.

25 If we live in the Spirit, let us also walk in the Spirit.

26 Let us not be desirous of vainglory, provoking one another and envying one another.

 ## Freedom in Christ

New International Version

5 It is for freedom that Christ has set us free. Stand firm, then, and do not let yourselves be burdened again by a yoke of slavery.

2 Mark my words! I, Paul, tell you that if you let yourselves be circumcised, Christ will be of no value to you at all. 3 Again I declare to every man who lets himself be circumcised that he is obligated to obey the whole law. 4 You who are trying to be justified by the law have been alienated from Christ; you have fallen away from grace. 5 For through the Spirit we eagerly await by faith the righteousness for which we hope. 6 For in Christ Jesus neither circumcision nor uncircumcision has any value. The only thing that counts is faith expressing itself through love.

7 You were running a good race. Who cut in on you to keep you from obeying the truth? 8 That kind of persuasion does not come from the one who calls you. 9 "A little yeast works through the whole batch of dough." 10 I am confident in the Lord that you will take no other view. The one who is throwing you into confusion, whoever that may be, will have to pay the penalty. 11 Brothers and sisters, if I am still preaching circumcision, why am I still being persecuted? In that case the offense of the cross has been abolished. 12 As for those agitators, I wish they would go the whole way and emasculate themselves!

Life by the Spirit

13 You, my brothers and sisters, were called to be free. But do not use your freedom to indulge the flesh[a]; rather, serve one another humbly in love. 14 For the entire law is fulfilled in keeping this one command: "Love your neighbor as yourself."[b] 15 If you bite and devour each other, watch out or you will be destroyed by each other.

16 So I say, walk by the Spirit, and you will not gratify the desires of the flesh. 17 For the flesh desires what is contrary to the Spirit, and the Spirit what is contrary to the flesh. They are in conflict with each other, so that you are not to do whatever[c] you want. 18 But if you are led by the Spirit, you are not under the law.

19 The acts of the flesh are obvious: sexual immorality, impurity and debauchery; 20 idolatry and witchcraft; hatred, discord, jealousy, fits of rage, selfish ambition, dissensions, factions 21 and envy; drunkenness, orgies, and the like. I warn you, as I did before, that those who live like this will not inherit the kingdom of God.

22 But the fruit of the Spirit is love, joy, peace, forbearance, kindness, goodness, faithfulness, 23 gentleness and self-control. Against such things there is no law. 24 Those who belong to Christ Jesus have crucified the flesh with its passions and desires. 25 Since we live by the Spirit, let us keep in step with the Spirit. 26 Let us not become conceited, provoking and envying each other.

[29/01/2023, 8:17:03 am] Dad:

The world and the church is full of deceit and hypocrisy

Jesus wondered if He would find faith on earth when He returns!

[29/01/2023, 8:17:30 am] Andrea:

Did he say that?

[29/01/2023, 8:19:27 am] Dad:

Luke 18 8

Luke 18:8

21st Century King James Version

8 I tell you that He will avenge them speedily. Nevertheless when the Son of Man cometh, shall He find faith on the earth?"

Luke 18:8

New International Version

8 I tell you, he will see that they get justice, and quickly. However, when the Son of Man comes, will he find faith on the earth?"

[29/01/2023, 8:24:25 am] Dad:

Read Jeremiah 17.9-10

God even regretted that He created human!

Jeremiah 17:9-10

21st Century King James Version

9 The heart is deceitful above all things, and desperately wicked; who can know it?

10 "I, the Lord, search the heart; I try the reins, even to give every man according to his ways, and according to the fruit of his doings."

New International Version

9 The heart is deceitful above all things

and beyond cure.

Who can understand it?

10 "I the Lord search the heart

and examine the mind,

to reward each person according to their conduct,

according to what their deeds deserve."

[30/01/2023, 2:04:21 pm] Dad:

Bola Worship Song Recommendation

Jesus I Love Calling Your Name - Shirley Caesar

Lyrics:

Jesus (Jesus)

Oh Jesus (Jesus)

Oh how I love

To call your name (calling your name)

Oh Jesus (Jesus)

Oh sweet Jesus (Jesus)

Everyday (everyday), uh huh, your name is the same

When my troubles surround me

And I didn't have to despair

Lord you told me

That you'll be right there

It seems like all my problems

Had just begun

I didn't have to worry no more

They were already won

Oh Jesus (Jesus)

Oh Jesus

Oh how I love

Calling your name

Ooh Jesus, Jesus (Jesus)

Sweet Jesus, Jesus (Jesus)

Oh every day, yes it is

Your name is the same

Yeah

I remember the time

When I felt so all alone

When I needed you Jesus

All I had to do was call

Sometimes in the morning

Sometimes late at night

But when I got off my knees Jesus

Everything was alright

Oh oh Jesus (Jesus)

My rose of Sharon

My lily of the valley

Calling your name

Ooh Jesus, Jesus my mountain mover (Jesus)

Everyday, yeah Jesus (every day)

Everyday is the same

Ooh, oh Jesus nobody but Jesus

Oh how I love I love I love

To call on your holy name, hey ey

Jesus, Jesus, nobody but Jesus, hey yey yey yeah

Everyday hallelujah your name is the same

Oh, oh oh, Jesus, Jesus

My mother Jesus, my father Jesus

I love, I love calling your name

Ooh come on Jesus

Come on Jesus

Come on Jesus

Come on Jesus

Everyday

Nobody but Jesus

[30/01/2023, 2:55:39 pm] Andrea:

Very nice

[30/01/2023, 2:55:46 pm] Andrea:

I haven't heard that before

[30/01/2023, 3:01:12 pm] Dad:

It had been my childhood song. I must have taught you growing up. It was the song in church yesterday that lifted my spirit

I am playing it all day

[30/01/2023, 3:15:27 pm] Dad:

I will sing it tomorrow after Niyi's birthday song

[30/01/2023, 3:54:40 pm] Andrea:

Can you sing?

[30/01/2023, 3:56:39 pm] Dad:

I was actually in the choir 1959 to 1963

[30/01/2023, 4:02:19 pm] Dad:

Dad had a church at the family house Ibadan

He played the organ and we all sang.

Andrea:

I love this one

Phil Wickham - How Great Thou Art

Lyrics:

Then sings my soul, my savior God, to thee

How great thou art

How great thou art

Then sings my soul, my savior God, to thee

How great thou art

How great thou art

Lets sing it one more time together

Then sings my soul, my savior God, to thee

How great thou art

How great thou art

Then sings my soul, my savior God, to thee

How great thou art

How great thou art

Phil Wickham - Great Things

Lyrics:

Come let us worship our King

Come let us bow at His feet

He has done great things

See what our Savior has done

See how His love overcomes

He has done great things

He has done great things

Oh, hero of Heaven

You conquered the grave

You free every captive and break every chain

Oh God, You have done great things

We dance in Your freedom, awake and alive

Oh Jesus, our Savior, Your name lifted high

Oh God, You have done great things

You've been faithful through every storm

You'll be faithful forevermore

You have done great things

And I know You will do it again

For Your promise is "Yes and amen"

You will do great things

God, You do great things

Oh, hero of Heaven, You conquered the grave

You free every captive and break every chain

Oh God, You have done great things

We dance in Your freedom, awake and alive

Oh Jesus, our Savior, Your name lifted high

Oh God, You have done great things

Hallelujah God, above it all

Hallelujah God, unshakable

Hallelujah, You have done great things

Hallelujah God, above it all

Hallelujah God, unshakable

Hallelujah, You have done great things

You've done great things

Oh, hero of Heaven, You conquered the grave

You free every captive and break every chain

Oh God, You have done great things

We dance in Your freedom, awake and alive

Oh Jesus, our Savior, Your name lifted high

Oh God, You have done great things

You have done great things

Oh God, You do great things

[30/01/2023, 8:51:08 pm] Dad:

Great song. Reminds me of Hillsong and one event

[30/01/2023, 8:56:24 pm] Andrea:

Exactly

[30/01/2023, 9:29:32 pm] Dad:

Good night God bless you all

[30/01/2023, 9:39:27 pm] Andrea:

Night Dad

[30/01/2023, 11:01:35 pm] Andrea:

Hey Dad, check out this story about Steve Harvey and how he got started at the Apollo. Today people want to be in control. I feel uneasy when I am not in control of things. What do you think about that?

[30/01/2023, 11:34:03 pm] Dad:

Amen. Thanks. This is good and inspirational

[31/01/2023, 5:04:59 am] Dad:

Wonderful message. Don't quit else it will never happen

God is never too late. He controls the times and seasons

My favorite scripture. Psalms 126 v 1

 Psalm 126

21st Century King James Version

126 When the Lord returned the captives to Zion, we were like them that dream.

2 Then was our mouth filled with laughter, and our tongue with singing. Then said they among the heathen, "The Lord hath done great things for them."

3 The Lord hath done great things for us, whereof we are glad.

4 Turn back our captivity, O Lord, as the streams in the South.

5 They that sow in tears shall reap in joy.

6 He that goeth forth and weepeth, bearing precious seed, shall doubtless come again with rejoicing, bringing his sheaves with him.

New International Version

A song of ascents.

1 When the Lord restored the fortunes of[a] Zion,

we were like those who dreamed.[b]

2 Our mouths were filled with laughter,

our tongues with songs of joy.

Then it was said among the nations,

"The Lord has done great things for them."

3 The Lord has done great things for us,

and we are filled with joy.

4 Restore our fortunes,[c] Lord,

like streams in the Negev.

5 Those who sow with tears

will reap with songs of joy.

6 Those who go out weeping,

carrying seed to sow,

will return with songs of joy,

carrying sheaves with them.

Fight My Battles | Josh Baldwin

Lyrics:

This is how I fight my battles

This is how I fight my battles

This is how I fight my battles

This is how I fight my battles

[Chorus]

It may look like I'm surrounded, but I'm surrounded by You

It may look like I'm surrounded, but I'm surrounded by You

It may look like I'm surrounded, but I'm surrounded by You

It may look like I'm surrounded, but I'm surrounded by You

[Verse]

This is how I fight my battles

This is how I fight my battles

This is how I fight my battles

This is how I fight my battles, mm

[Chorus]

It may look like I'm surrounded, but I'm surrounded by You

It may look like I'm surrounded, but I'm surrounded by You

It may look like I'm surrounded, but I'm surrounded by You

It may look like I'm surrounded, but I'm surrounded by You

It may look like I'm surrounded, but I'm surrounded by You

It may look like I'm surrounded, but I'm surrounded by You

It may look like I'm surrounded, but I'm surrounded by You

It may look like I'm surrounded, but I'm surrounded by You

Rock of Ages, cleft for me

Let me hide, let me hide

Rock of Ages, cleft for me

Let me hide, let me hide

Let me hide myself in Thee

[Verse]

This is how I fight my battles, mm

This is how I fight my battles

This is how I fight my battles, yeah

This is how I fight my battles

Question 3: [03/02/2023, 2:36:46 pm] Dad:

As you were growing up did you enjoy going to Church with me?

Question 4: Dad:

How did you feel dressing up on Sundays?

Question 5: Dad:

What were your lasting memories and impressions?

[03/02/2023, 2:49:50 pm]

Question 6. Dad:

Did you ever keep part of the offering money I gave you or you joyfully dropped all In the offering bag?

I heard that many children played pranks with theirs

[03/02/2023, 2:50:42 pm] Andrea:

That's funny!

[08/02/2023, 6:11:09 am] Andrea:

I remember going to that big Anglican Church in Kano. What was its name again? St. George maybe? It had a big compound. I remember us going as a family and liking that. Then there was always a nice activity afterwards like going to Baguda to swim or visiting friends like the Kosokos. My memories were that Sundays were always relaxed with things that I enjoyed in the whole day including church.

I remember Awuujola being in church. Her and I did a collection once and my wrappa fell down. I remember the missionary Marie that used to go into villages with puppets made from paper mache to explain about cholera and drinking dirty water. We helped make puppets.

When I was a teenager and came on holidays I don't remember enjoying those churches as much. There seemed too much pressure on what I was wearing. I was young and wasn't always good at knowing. I remember you getting clothes made for me which I would wear. I remember not really understanding much they were saying and being bored. The services were long and made me feel sleepy. Still Sundays were a nice day and we would go and eat lunch at Kano club. I liked that part.

I always put my offering money in. I don't think it ever occurred to me not to. I think I quite liked doing that and feeling a sense of belonging. I never really understood much of what was being said but those early memories created good habits and a positive association with church.

 Hebrews 10:24-25

21st Century King James Version

24 and let us consider one another to provoke unto love and to good works,

25 not forsaking the assembling of ourselves together, as is the manner of some, but exhorting one another, and so much the more as ye see the Day approaching.

 Hebrews 10:24-25

New International Version

24 And let us consider how we may spur one another on toward love and good deeds, 25 not giving up meeting together, as some are in the habit of doing, but encouraging one another—and all the more as you see the Day approaching.

[03/02/2023, 2:51:36 pm] Dad:

Ok

[05/02/2023, 7:24:26 am] Dad:

Good morning all. It is well Glory

Happy Sunday.

Andrea:

Happy Sunday Dad!

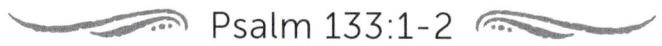

Psalm 133:1-2

21st Century King James Version

133 Behold, how good and how pleasant it is for brethren to dwell together in unity!

2 It is like the precious ointment upon the head that ran down upon the beard, even Aaron's beard that went down to the skirts of his garments.

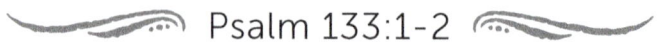

Psalm 133:1-2

New International Version

Psalm 133

A song of ascents. Of David.

1 How good and pleasant it is

when God's people live together in unity!

2 It is like precious oil poured on the head,

running down on the beard,

running down on Aaron's beard,

down on the collar of his robe.

Worship Song
Recommendation

Graves Into Gardens

By Elevation Worship

[Verse 1]

I searched the world

But it couldn't fill me

Man's empty praise and treasures that fade are never enough

Then You came along

And put me back together

And every desire is now satisfied

Here in Your love (Hey)

[Chorus]

Oh, there's nothing better than You

There's nothing better than You

Lord, there's nothing

Nothing is better than You

[Interlude]

Oh, yes, I know it's true

Come on, stand up

[Verse 2]

I'm not afraid

To show You my weakness

My failures and flaws

Lord, You've seem them all

And You still call me friend

'Cause the God of the mountain

Is the God of the valley

There's not a place Your mercy and grace

Won't find me again

[Chorus]

Oh, there's nothing better than You

There's nothing (Oh) better than You

Lord, there's nothing

Nothing is better than You (I know it's true)

Oh, there's nothing better than You (Somebody testify)

There's nothing better than you (Oh, there's nothing, nothing, no)

Lord, there's nothing

Nothing is better than You

[Interlude]

Faith has made a way for you all so you can sing this

Come on, tear the roof off

[Bridge]

You turn mourning to dancing

You give beauty for ashes

You turn shame into glory

You're the only one who can (Come on)

You turn mourning to dancing

You give beauty for ashes

You turn shame into glory (Tell 'em now)

You're the only one who can (Let's turn the graves)

You turn graves into gardens

You turn bones into armies

You turn seas into highways

You're the only one who can (He's the only Lord)

You're the only one who can

[Chorus]

Oh, there's nothing (Come on, choir) better than You

There's nothing better than You

Lord, there's nothing

Nothing is better than You (Search and not found)

Oh, there's nothing better than You

There's nothing better than you (Oh, there's nothing)

Lord, there's nothing

Nothing is better than You

[Interlude]

Oh, come on, let's turn our graves into a garden, say:

[Bridge]

You turn graves into gardens

You turn bones into armies

You turn seas into highways

You're the only one who can (Turn to graves)

You turn graves into gardens (Turn your bones into an army)

You turn bones into armies (He's makin' waves through the seas)

You turn seas into highways

You're the only one who can

You're the only one who can (Praise to the Lord)

You're the only one who can

You're the only one who can

[Interlude]

Somebody give Him praise in this house

Woo

I don't think we're finished yet, come on

I think He's turning some things over tonight

You turn my mourning into dancing, come on:

[Bridge]

You turn mourning to dancing (Yeah)

You give beauty for ashes (Shame into glory)

You turn shame into glory (Say it, the only name)

You're the only one who can (Oh, He's turnin' my grave)

You turn graves into gardens

You turn bones into armies (He's makin' waves through the seas)

You turn seas into highways (You're the only)

You're the only one who can (Come on, one more time, you turn my grave into a garden)

You turn graves into gardens (You're resurrectin' bones)

You turn bones into armies (You're makin' waves through my sea)

You turn seas into highways (Shout it out, You're the only)

You're the only one who can (You're the only)

You're the only one who can (You're the only)

You're the only one who can

[Outro]

Jesus, You're the only one

Come on, give Him one more shout of praise

Question 7:

What do you do when you are afraid of something that hasn't happened yet but might?

[01/02/2023, 9:29:46 am] Dad:

Good morning all Happy new month

[01/02/2023, 12:29:34 pm] Andrea:

Good morning Dad. Just spoken to my boss. Redundancies have been announced and my job is safe!

[01/02/2023, 12:45:17 pm] Dad:

Our God is faithful

He will not leave us nor forsake us

He watches over us for good

He will not put us to shame

Hallelujah

[01/02/2023, 12:47:02 pm] Andrea:

Amen!

[01/02/2023, 12:48:29 pm] Dad:

And a thunderous AMEN

 Proverbs 23:7-10

21st Century King James Version

7 for as he thinketh in his heart, so is he. "Eat and drink," saith he to thee, but his heart is not with thee.

Proverbs 23:7-10

New International Version

7 for he is the kind of person

who is always thinking about the cost.[a]

"Eat and drink," he says to you,

but his heart is not with you.

Worship Song Recommendation

Way Maker | Steffany Gretzinger | John Wilds

Lyrics:

You are here, moving in our midst

I worship You

I worship You

You are here, working in this place

I worship You

I worship You

You are here, moving in our midst

I worship You

I worship You

You are here, working in this place

I worship You

I worship You

You are

Way maker, miracle worker, promise keeper

Light in the darkness

My God, that is who You are

You are

Way maker, miracle worker, promise keeper

Light in the darkness

My God, that is who You are

You are here, touching every heart

I worship You

I worship You

You are here, healing every heart

Healing every heart

Oh, I worship You

Jesus, I worship You

You're turning lives around

You are here, oh, turning lives around

I worship You

I worship You

You mended every heart

You are here, and You are mending every heart

I worship You, yeah

I worship You

And You are

Way maker, miracle worker, promise keeper

Light in the darkness

My God, that is who You are

Yeah You're the way maker

Way maker, miracle worker, promise keeper

Light in the darkness

My God, that is who You are

Yeah sing it again You are, yeah

Way maker, miracle worker, promise keeper

Light in the darkness

My God, that is who You are

Oh it's who You are, Jesus, yeah

Way maker, miracle worker, promise keeper

Light in the darkness

My God, that is who You are

Sing that is who You are

Oh, that is who You are

And that is who You are

Oh, and that is who You are

That is who You are

Lord Jesus, that is who You are

That is who You are (oh, He lifts you up)

That is who You are

That is who You are

My Jesus, yeah

Miracle worker, promise keeper

Light in the darkness

My God, that is who You are

Yes it is yeah, it's who You are

Way maker, miracle worker, promise keeper

Light in the darkness (hey)

My God, that is who You are

Let's sing this together

Even when I don't see it, come on, even when

Even when I don't see it, You're working

Even when I don't feel it, You're working

You never stop, You never stop working

You never stop, You never stop working (come on)

And even when I don't see it, You're working

Even when I don't feel it, You're working

You never stop, You never stop working

You never stop, You never stop working (oh)

Even when I don't see it, You're working

Even when I don't feel it, You're working

You never stop, You never stop working

You never stop (yeah, oh), You never stop working

Even when I don't see it, You're working

Even when I don't feel it (yeah), You're working

You never stop, You never stop working

You never stop, You never stop working (You're the way maker, yeah-yeah)

Way maker, miracle worker, promise keeper

Light in the darkness

My God, that is who You are

Yeah, yeah

Way maker, miracle worker, promise keeper

Light in the darkness

My God, that is who You are

Sing that is who You are

Oh, that is who You are

That is who You are

Oh and, that is who You are

That is who You are

Yeah, and that is who You are, yeah

That is who You are

Oh, that is who You are

That is who You are

Oh it's who You are, now Jesus

Way maker, miracle worker, promise keeper

Light in the darkness

My God, that is who You are

You are

Way maker, miracle worker, promise keeper

Light in the darkness

My God, that is who You are

Oh, His name is above

His name is above depression

His name is above loneliness

Oh, His name is above disease

His name is above cancer

His name is above every other name

Yes it is

That is who You are

(That is who You are)

That is who You are

(That is who You are) Jesus

And that is who You are

(That is who You are)

Oh, I know that is who You are

That is who You are

Question 8

[08/02/2023, 7:11:47 am] Dad:

Nice to hear good news about the new consultancy. God will increase you In Jesus Name. I reckon that you pay 10 percent of your 1st pay as Tithe. God will multiply it back to you a thousand fold In Jesus Name.

[08/02/2023, 8:10:18 am] Andrea:

I have never done regular 10% tithing. I give when I can financially and in the meantime give my time and talents. I need to make sure I make time for that in the busyness of life. Do you think it's always necessary to tithe? Do you think the biblical 10% has been taken too literally and it's the concept that counts? Do you think giving your time and talents are an acceptable substitute for giving money? Do you think churches sometimes show favouritism to those who give more?

I remember being in Nigerian churches with three or four collections! Do you think there can be too much asking for money?

What do you think the money should be spent on?

What do you think about rich churches and extremely wealthy Pastors while people all around them are in extreme poverty and suffering?

[08/02/2023, 8:54:12 am] Dad:

Tithing started in the old testament. Abraham paid tithe. Genesis 14 20. We are His descendants

Malachi 3 10 puts a curse on him that doesn't pay.

 Genesis 14:20

21st Century King James Version

20 and blessed be the Most High God, who hath delivered thine enemies into thy hand." And he gave him tithes of all.

Genesis 14:20

New International Version

20 And praise be to God Most High,

who delivered your enemies into your hand."

Then Abram gave him a tenth of everything.

Malachi 3:10

21st Century King James Version

10 Bring ye all the tithes into the storehouse, that there may be meat in Mine house, and put Me to the proof now herewith," saith the Lord of hosts, "if I will not open to you the windows of heaven and pour you out a blessing, that there shall not be room enough to receive it.

Malachi 3:10

New International Version

10 Bring the whole tithe into the storehouse, that there may be food in my house. Test me in this," says the Lord Almighty, "and see if I will not throw open the floodgates of heaven and pour out so much blessing that there will not be room enough to store it.

Jesus mentioned tithe in the new testament but didn't condemn it. **Matthew 23 23-24**

Matthew 23:23-24

21st Century King James Version

23 "Woe unto you, scribes and Pharisees, hypocrites! For ye pay tithe of mint and anise and cummin, and have omitted the weightier matters of the law: judgment, mercy, and faith. These ought ye to have done and not to leave the other undone.

24 Ye blind guides, who strain out a gnat and swallow a camel!

Matthew 23:23-24

New International Version

23 "Woe to you, teachers of the law and Pharisees, you hypocrites! You give a tenth of your spices—mint, dill and cumin. But you have neglected the more important matters of the law—justice, mercy and faithfulness. You should have practiced the latter, without neglecting the former. 24 You blind guides! You strain out a gnat but swallow a camel.

I was a faithful tither for a long time but I stopped unfortunately. It was either hardship or the devil.

[08/02/2023, 9:35:14 am] Dad:

Other offerings or sacrifices or services in the church cannot replace tithing. Tithing is a financial covenant between you and God.

[08/02/2023, 9:43:42 am] Dad:

Tithes are for the priests and Ministers of the church. They had no salaries then.

There is a lot of abuse in the house of God today. Greed, covetous living and discriminations

The Bible commands us not to judge our religious leaders. God judges them. We pray for them.

[08/02/2023, 10:28:22 am] Dad:

Too much collections in Churches are detrimental to church growth. The money should be spent to support the poor, the widows and orphans. It is Biblical James 1 27

James 1:27

21st Century King James Version

27 Pure religion, undefiled before God and the Father, is this: to visit the fatherless and widows in their affliction, and to keep himself unspotted from the world.

James 1:27

New International Version

27 Religion that God our Father accepts as pure and faultless is this: to look after orphans and widows in their distress and to keep oneself from being polluted by the world.

Worship Song
Recommendation

How Great Thou Art

Song by Carrie Underwood

Lyrics:

… Oh Lord, my God

When I, in awesome wonder

Consider all the worlds Thy hands have made

I see the stars, I hear the rolling thunder

Thy power throughout the universe displayed

… Then sings my soul, my Savior God to Thee

How great Thou art, how great Thou art

Then sings my soul, my Savior God to Thee

How great Thou art, how great Thou art

… And when I think that God, His Son not sparing

Sent Him to die, I scarce can take it in

That on the cross, my burden gladly bearing

He bled and died to take away my sin

… Then sings my soul, my Savior God to Thee

How great Thou art, how great Thou art

Then sings my soul, my Savior God to Thee

How great Thou art, how great Thou art

… When Christ shall come, with shout of acclamation

And take me home, what joy shall fill my heart

Then I shall bow, in humble adoration

And then proclaim, my God, how great Thou art

… Then sings my soul, my Savior God to Thee

How great Thou art, how great Thou art

Then sings my soul, my Savior God to Thee

How great Thou art, how great Thou art

How great Thou art, how great Thou art

Question 9:

[08/02/2023, 8:12:14 am] Andrea:

I'm reading about the devastation in Turkey and Syria after a catastrophic earthquake that killed 6,000 people or more.

What do you think when people say if there was a God he would not allow these things to happen?

[08/02/2023, 8:25:53 am] Dad:

Very interesting questions

Jack or India asked me the last question in one of our Bible studies

God is Omni Magnificent. He created good and evil. He gives life and takes life. But He is not the author of confusion. He does afflict but not deliberately.

He is Sovereign and does what pleases Him.

His thoughts for us are for good and not evil to give us hope **Jeremiah 29 v 11**

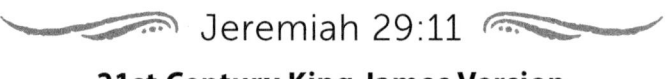 Jeremiah 29:11

21st Century King James Version

11 For I know the thoughts that I think toward you, saith the Lord, thoughts of peace and not of evil, to give you an expected end.

 Jeremiah 29:11

New International Version

11 For I know the plans I have for you," declares the Lord, "plans to prosper you and not to harm you, plans to give you hope and a future.

His wish is for us to prosper and be in health even as our souls prosper **3 John 2**

John 3:2

21st Century King James Version

2 The same came to Jesus by night and said unto Him, "Rabbi, we know that thou art a teacher come from God; for no man can do these miracles that thou doest, unless God be with him."

John 3:2

New International Version

2 He came to Jesus at night and said, "Rabbi, we know that you are a teacher who has come from God. For no one could perform the signs you are doing if God were not with him."

Romans 8:1 says a child of God cannot be cursed or condemned.

Romans 8:1

21st Century King James Version

8 There is therefore now no condemnation for those who are in Christ Jesus, who walk not according to the flesh, but according to the Spirit.

Romans 8:1

New International Version

Life Through the Spirit

8 Therefore, there is now no condemnation for those who are in Christ Jesus,

Thank you
Aunty Niyi

Question 10:

Does it work to join faith and pray collectively?

Please assure me that you have time to check these scriptures

Faith cometh by hearing and hearing the word of God

[08/02/2023, 11:03:51 am] Dad:

I am done with typing for a while. Going for a rest and preparing for tomorrow and Friday. No banks are open. They are being attacked for not disbursing cash. People are hungry and angry. You talk of positivity!

We are blessed only

[08/02/2023, 11:12:45 am] Dad:

It is trade by Batter now as in slave age

Give me some meat and I can give you Gari.

[08/02/2023, 12:38:02 pm] Dad:

We have cash in hand for the tests tomorrow. We will go by faith that the Pharmacy accepts a bank transfer for the Chemo and bone therapy. Please join your faith with ours.

Andrea:

Does that work Dad?

Dad:

In Mark 6 Jesus could not perform a miracle in his own home because of the unbelief of the people. There is faith to heal and faith to the healed. Both are needed. If God grants you the faith to heal you you must also have the faith to receive the healing otherwise it's useless.

Mark 6:5-6

21st Century King James Version

5 And He could do no mighty works there, except that He laid His hands upon a few sick folk, and healed them.

6 And He marveled because of their unbelief. And He went round about the villages teaching.

Mark 6:5-6

New International Version

5 He could not do any miracles there, except lay his hands on a few sick people and heal them. 6 He was amazed at their lack of faith.

Jesus Sends Out the Twelve

Then Jesus went around teaching from village to village.

Andrea:

How does that answer the question?

Dad:

If we are praying together for instance but you do not believe in the power of prayer then it may not work for you. The Bible says in Matthew 18:18 if two believe in a particular thing it will be done to them. That is why it says that two are better than one. So if I am praying for you but you don't believe in prayer I am wasting my time. God listens to you and answers prayer.

[05/05/2023, 7:33:39 pm] Andrea:

On Monday Jack has an American exam in Harrogate. I'm just looking at the awful drive!

[05/05/2023, 7:34:12 pm] Andrea:

He swims on Sunday evening and finishes at 7pm so that's the soonest we can leave.

[05/05/2023, 10:00:45 pm] Dad:

You are all covered by the blood of Jesus. He will succeed in both

Matthew 18:18-19

21st Century King James Version

18 Verily I say unto you, whatsoever ye shall bind on earth shall be bound in Heaven; and so whatsoever ye shall loose on earth shall be loosed in Heaven.

19 "Again I say unto you, that if two of you shall agree on earth concerning anything that they shall ask, it shall be done for them by My Father who is in Heaven.

Matthew 18:18-19

New International Version

18 "Truly I tell you, whatever you bind on earth will be[a] bound in heaven, and whatever you loose on earth will be[b] loosed in heaven.

19 "Again, truly I tell you that if two of you on earth agree about anything they ask for, it will be done for them by my Father in heaven.

What if you are praying for people who don't believe or who aren't Christian's yet?

Dad:

That is the miracle of God. He sends rain down on the just and the unjust. That is the grace of God as the creator of all human beings both Christians and nonchristians. His grace is sufficient for all of us.

Andrea:

So is it then a waste of time to pray for someone who doesn't believe?

Dad:

No. Your prayer can convert them and make them believe. Remember the thief crucified with Jesus. Jesus prayed for him and he went to heaven.

I was just thinking about Rejoice in the Lord Always: **Philippians 4 4**

Philippians 4

21st Century King James Version

4 Rejoice in the Lord always; and again I say, "Rejoice!"

5 Let your moderation be known to all men. The Lord is at hand.

6 Fret not about anything, but in everything, by prayer and supplication with thanksgiving, let your requests be made known unto God.

Philippians 4

New International Version

4 Rejoice in the Lord always. I will say it again: Rejoice!

5 Let your gentleness be evident to all. The Lord is near.

6 Do not be anxious about anything, but in every situation, by prayer and petition, with thanksgiving, present your requests to God.

7 And the peace of God, which transcends all understanding, will guard your hearts and your minds in Christ Jesus.

Andrea:

This reminds me of Rock of ages. You love that song! Even when we may feel like we are alone, it reminds us that God is always by our side and will never abandon us. He is our light in the dark and our rock that we can always stand on.

Rock of Ages

by Augustus Toplady

Lyrics:

Rock of Ages, cleft for me,

Let me hide myself in Thee;

Let the water and the blood,

From Thy wounded side which flowed,

Be of sin the double cure,

Save from wrath and make me pure.

Not the labor of my hands

Can fulfill Thy law's demands;

Could my zeal no respite know,

Could my tears forever flow,

All for sin could not atone;

Thou must save, and Thou alone.

Nothing in my hand I bring,

Simply to Thy cross I cling;

Naked, come to Thee for dress;

Helpless, look to Thee for grace;

Foul, I to the fountain fly;

Wash me, Savior, or I die.

While I draw this fleeting breath,

When my eyes shall close in death,

When I rise to worlds unknown,

And behold Thee on Thy throne,

Rock of Ages, cleft for me,

Let me hide myself in Thee.

Question 11:

I have been made unemployed Dad. Why does this keep happening to me?

[08/02/2023, 12:44:32 pm] Andrea:

I just got news that my job is not safe after all. So dealing with that.

[08/02/2023, 12:53:07 pm] Dad:

Why and how the sudden twist? God is on the Throne

He will reverse the irreversible In Jesus Name.

[08/02/2023, 1:48:18 pm] Andrea:

Cost cutting. Let's see.

[08/02/2023, 2:02:50 pm] Dad:

It is a global phenomenon. God controls the times and seasons. If one door is shut a bigger one He opens.

[08/02/2023, 2:03:56 pm] Andrea:

Amen.

[08/02/2023, 2:32:48 pm] Dad:

Please let not your heart be troubled. Simply cast your burden on God

[08/02/2023, 3:14:11 pm] Andrea:

Thanks Dad.

Dad:

You can't wait to be happy. **Isaiah 60 1-2**. You must arise!

 Isaiah 60:1-2

21st Century King James Version

60 Arise, shine, for thy light is come, and the glory of the Lord is risen upon thee.

2 For behold, the darkness shall cover the earth and gross darkness the people; but the Lord shall arise upon thee, and His glory shall be seen upon thee.

 Isaiah 60:1-2

New International Version

The Glory of Zion

60 "Arise, shine, for your light has come,

and the glory of the Lord rises upon you.

2 See, darkness covers the earth

and thick darkness is over the peoples,

but the Lord rises upon you

and his glory appears over you.

Dad:

Look also at **John 14 v1**

21st Century King James Version

14 "Let not your heart be troubled. Ye believe in God; believe also in Me.

2 In My Father's house are many mansions; if it were not so, I would have told you. I go to prepare a place for you.

3 And if I go and prepare a place for you, I will come again and receive you unto Myself, that where I am, there ye may be also.

4 And whither I go ye know, and the way ye know."

5 Thomas said unto Him, "Lord, we know not whither Thou goest; and how can we know the way?"

 John 14

New International Version

Jesus Comforts His Disciples

14 "Do not let your hearts be troubled. You believe in God[a]; believe also in me.

2 My Father's house has many rooms; if that were not so, would I have told you that I am going there to prepare a place for you?

3 And if I go and prepare a place for you, I will come back and take you to be with me that you also may be where I am.

4 You know the way to the place where I am going."

Question 12:

How do you lift yourself up when you feel down and helpless?

Andrea:

Expectation is the breeding ground of miracles. Come to God with expectation.

Rejoicing in the Lord is a theme that should be part of everyday life. Find a way that works for you. Prayer, conversations, bible study, debate with your children or worship songs all count!

Happy - something good has to happen for you to be happy, but to rejoice you are making a decision to rejoice in the Lord and in what he has done and who he is. Trust that he is always leading and guiding. Rejoicing is an act of faith that shows HIS spirit lives in you

Isaiah 61:10. Don't let your feelings lead you. Be led by the spirit of God.

 Isaiah 61:10

21st Century King James Version

10 I will greatly rejoice in the Lord; my soul shall be joyful in my God. For He hath clothed me with the garments of salvation; He hath covered me with the robe of righteousness, as a bridegroom decketh himself with ornaments, and as a bride adorneth herself with her jewels.

New International Version

10 I delight greatly in the Lord;

my soul rejoices in my God.

For he has clothed me with garments of salvation

and arrayed me in a robe of his righteousness,

as a bridegroom adorns his head like a priest,

and as a bride adorns herself with her jewels.

[10/02/2023, 4:19:13 pm] Dad:

I am prepared to face the about 5 harsh day post chemo period with prayer and aggression.

God will back me up and I have laid down the drugs from confusion to nausea to loss of appetite to insomnia to blood pressure fluctuation etc. Just keep me in your prayers

[10/02/2023, 4:48:34 pm] Andrea:

Of course I do. This is the last one Dad. You're almost through it.

[10/02/2023, 4:49:30 pm] Andrea:

You have got through 100% of your bad days! That's a good success rate. You will get through this.

[10/02/2023, 5:10:15 pm] Dad:

Amen and amen my beloved daughter. God bless you.

[10/02/2023, 9:27:49 pm] Dad:

I have some tests and consultations for next week to determine the efficiency of the treatments so far.

May God crown all your efforts and sacrifices with success

[11/02/2023, 6:29:45 am] Dad:

Good morning daughter How was your night?

We are up hail and healthy. Glory.

God will watch over you for good today and forever In Jesus Name.

[11/02/2023, 6:30:13 am] Andrea:

Jack is sick. I'm just rushing around. How are you feeling?

[11/02/2023, 6:36:14 am] Dad:

God will heal Jack. Please lay your hands on him and decree that the healing power of the lord will fall on him now in Jesus Name.

I am fine. Longer than usual in bed. Next 5 days crucial for prayer,rest and drugs

Thanks for standing firmly by us.

God bless you

[11/02/2023, 3:14:35 pm] Dad:

Good afternoon daughter. How are things with you and my grandchildren?

Please cheer up

It is a new day

The brightness of our rising shall attract greatness and all round blessings for The LORD.

Better days are coming for us

Rejoice and be glad

Happy Sunday

Worship Song
Recommendation

Hillsong. Jason Ingram

King Of Kings

VERSE 1

In the darkness we were waiting

Without hope without light

Till from heaven You came running

There was mercy in Your eyes

To fulfil the law and prophets

To a virgin came the Word

From a throne of endless glory

To a cradle in the dirt

CHORUS

Praise the Father

Praise the Son

Praise the Spirit three in one

God of glory

Majesty

Praise forever to the King of Kings

VERSE 2

To reveal the kingdom coming

And to reconcile the lost

To redeem the whole creation

You did not despise the cross

For even in Your suffering

You saw to the other side

Knowing this was our salvation

Jesus for our sake You died

VERSE 3

And the morning that You rose

All of heaven held its breath

Till that stone was moved for good

For the Lamb had conquered death

And the dead rose from their tombs

And the angels stood in awe

For the souls of all who'd come

To the Father are restored

VERSE 4

And the Church of Christ was born

Then the Spirit lit the flame

Now this gospel truth of old

Shall not kneel shall not faint

By His blood and in His Name

In His freedom I am free

For the love of Jesus Christ

Who has resurrected me

Question 13:

Dad: Sometimes people see suffering, as we currently have in Nigeria with people being warned not to use ATM machines and food and diesel scarce. All this while others seem to thrive in abundance. How do we handle what seems like such injustice?

Andrea:

I know what you mean but I think that when people have fraudulently obtained that wealth or are relishing without ample consideration for those suffering all around them, God sees that. They will pay the price at some point. Look at us Dad. We are not rich but you are still alive after cancer throughout your body. Would we not choose that over any mansion? I know I would.

Dad:

The bible says this: The integrity of the upright shall guide them: but the perverseness of transgressors shall destroy them. **Proverbs 11:3**

 Proverbs 11:3

21st Century King James Version

3 The integrity of the upright shall guide them, but the perverseness of transgressors shall destroy them.

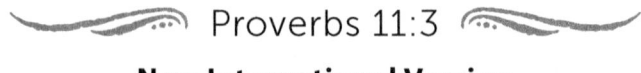 Proverbs 11:3

New International Version

3 The integrity of the upright guides them,

but the unfaithful are destroyed by their duplicity.

Questions 14 & 15:

Is saying "by God's Grace" overrated?

[13/06/2017, 4:24:54 pm] Dad:

See you tomorrow by God's grace

[13/06/2017, 4:25:48 pm] Andrea:

If you overslept would that be God's fault or human error???!

[13/06/2017, 4:30:46 pm] Dad:

Everything works together for good to them that love God and are called according to His purpose. **Rom. 8:28**

 Romans 8:28

21st Century King James Version

28 And we know that all things work together for good to those who love God, to those who are the called according to His purpose.

 Romans 8:28

New International Version

28 And we know that in all things God works for the good of those who love him, who[a] have been called according to his purpose.

[13/06/2017, 4:32:29 pm] Andrea:

James 2:14-17!

[13/06/2017, 4:33:56 pm] Andrea:

And even better **James 2:18** "I will show you my faith by my works"!

 James 2:14-17

21st Century King James Version

14 What doth it profit, my brethren, though a man say he hath faith, and hath not works? Can faith save him?

15 If a brother or sister be naked and destitute of daily food,

16 and one of you say unto them, "Depart in peace; be ye warmed and filled," without giving them those things which are needful to the body, what doth it profit?

17 Even so faith, if it hath not works, is dead, being alone.

 James 2:14-17

New International Version

Faith and Deeds

14 What good is it, my brothers and sisters, if someone claims to have faith but has no deeds? Can such faith save them? 15 Suppose a brother or a sister is without clothes and daily food. 16 If one of you says to them, "Go in peace; keep warm and well fed," but does nothing about their physical needs, what good is it? 17 In the same way, faith by itself, if it is not accompanied by action, is dead.

[13/06/2017, 4:38:22 pm] Andrea:

If we look at the meaning of grace ... the interpretations are things like Divine Intervention and unmerited Divine assistant. **Have people made the use of "by God's Grace" too commonplace? Do we need Gods grace for everything or is God's Grace reserved for when we are in a difficult situation that requires it? For the day to day simple things do we simply walk in faith knowing we are protected and loved?**

[13/06/2017, 4:38:26 pm] Dad:

Sometimes obstacles are put in our way to preserve us!

[13/06/2017, 4:40:40 pm] Andrea:

I agree! However those obstacles have not occurred yet and I believe (in faith) that they won't occur. If they do, I will then ask for God's Grace! In the meantime I will just joyful go about my travels!! 🐨

[13/06/2017, 4:44:04 pm] Dad:

You are absolutely correct. When God says NO to any of our requests it is still an answered prayer

[13/06/2017, 4:45:19 pm] Andrea:

So should we always say "I'm getting on the bus/going to school/waking up the next morning"... by God's Grace?

[13/06/2017, 4:45:47 pm] Andrea:

Do we require Devine intervention for these everyday things?

[13/06/2017, 4:47:57 pm] Dad:

That is the commandment in James 4:15

[13/06/2017, 4:57:21 pm] Andrea:

My view is that within the context of the other versus before and after this one, it means not that we literally need to say it out loud but that we need to acknowledge God as the keeper of our plan.

[13/06/2017, 5:29:23 pm] Dad:

You are correct also. But Rom 10:10 says that with the mouth confession is made unto salvation!

 Romans 10:10

21st Century King James Version

10 For with the heart man believeth unto righteousness, and with the mouth confession is made unto salvation.

 Romans 10:10

New International Version

10 For it is with your heart that you believe and are justified, and it is with your mouth that you profess your faith and are saved.

[13/06/2017, 6:18:35 pm] Andrea:

Ha!

[13/06/2017, 9:19:19 pm] Dad:

Sleeping early. Good night

[13/06/2017, 10:41:53 pm] Andrea:

See you at 7am.

[14/06/2017, 4:39:12 am] Dad:

Amen

Question 16:

Do you think it's true that difficulties draw you closer to God?

[09/05/2019, 3:45:41 pm] Dad:

That is a testimony

Your difficult time must have drawn you nearer to God. This is also a testimony.

I am sure that your perception of life is different now.

[09/05/2019, 5:42:38 pm] Dad:

Listen to Blessed Assurance

[09/05/2019, 8:03:49 pm] Andrea:

Nice song

[09/05/2019, 8:26:36 pm] Dad:

I hope you listened to the chorus: this my story

[09/05/2019, 8:45:01 pm] Andrea:

I know it well

[09/05/2019, 9:25:25 pm] Dad:

Good night. God bless

[09/05/2019, 9:26:50 pm] Andrea:

Night Dad

Romans 5:3-5

21st Century King James Version

3 And not only so, but we glory in tribulations also, knowing that tribulation worketh patience;

4 and patience, experience; and experience, hope;

5 and hope maketh not ashamed, because the love of God is shed abroad in our hearts by the Holy Ghost who is given unto us.

Romans 5:3-5

New International Version

3 Not only so, but we[a] also glory in our sufferings, because we know that suffering produces perseverance;

4 perseverance, character; and character, hope.

5 And hope does not put us to shame, because God's love has been poured out into our hearts through the Holy Spirit, who has been given to us.

Blessed Assurance

Song by Elevation Worship

Lyrics:

Blessed assurance, Jesus is mine

O what a foretaste of glory divine

Heir of salvation, purchase of God

Born of His Spirit, washed in His blood

Perfect submission, all is at rest

I in my Savior am happy and blessed

Watching and waiting, looking above

Filled with His goodness, lost in His love

This is my story, this is my song

Praising my Savior all the day long

This is my story, this is my song

Praising my Savior all the day long

Oh what a Savior, wonderful Jesus

Oh what a Savior, wonderful Jesus

Oh what a Savior, wonderful Jesus

Oh what a Savior, wonderful Jesus

Oh what a Savior, wonderful Jesus

Oh what a Savior, wonderful Jesus

Oh what a Savior, wonderful Jesus

Oh what a Savior, wonderful Jesus

Death could not hold You, You are victorious

Praise to the risen King

Death could not hold You, You are victorious

Praise to the risen King!

Oh what a Savior, wonderful Jesus

Oh what a Savior, wonderful Jesus

Oh what a Savior, wonderful Jesus

Oh what a Savior!

Wonderful Savior!

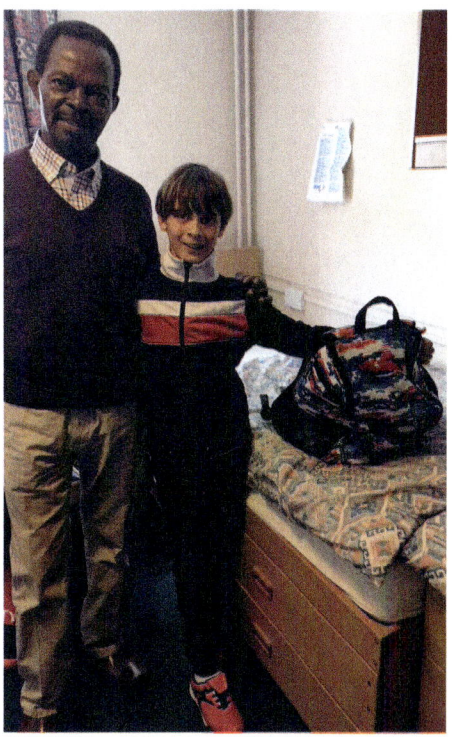

Question 17:

How do you face a difficult situation on your own?

When I had to face a very difficult situation on my own, I asked my Dad how to face it. This is what he said.

[08/10/2019, 4:33:31 am] Dad:

Morning daughter. Today I pray that God will lift your burdens, bless your home and grant you the desires of your heart In Jesus Name.

[08/10/2019, 8:06:34 am] Andrea:

Thank you Daddy. That was needed. In court tomorrow. Really dreading it.

[08/10/2019, 8:46:29 am] Dad:

Trust God to defend you.

There is no sorrow that the world brings our way that the heavens cannot contain.

[08/10/2019, 8:52:57 am] Dad:

Let God's will be done. This is my prayer for you

There are so many devices in the hearts of men but only the counsel of The Lord will prevail

Whichever way it turns out, don't forget to give thanks to God and receive His grace and strength to move on.

Even if no one goes with you to the Court, you are Not alone! God is with you. He will never leave you nor forsake you In Jesus Name.

[08/10/2019, 9:00:43 am] Andrea:

Thanks Dad. He is all I need and has truly been my salvation. My plan is to walk in humbly, ask nicely and walk out grateful... no matter what is said.

[08/10/2019, 9:03:39 am] Dad:

God will go with you and back you up In Jesus Name

[09/10/2019, 5:49:53 am] Dad:

Morning daughter.

Do not fear. Do not tremble. Do not be discouraged

God has not given you the spirit of fear but of boldness, love and a sound mind. So go in this might of yours.

God's Covenant of peace is released on you and His perfect will is done In Jesus Name.

[09/10/2019, 5:56:14 am] Dad:

Gods favour will overshadow you. He will be your strength. He will speak for you In Jesus Name.

[09/10/2019, 6:06:20 am] Dad:

Please read **Deuteronomy 31:6** and convert it to your prayers as you go

[09/10/2019, 12:00:38 pm] Andrea:

Thank you Dad

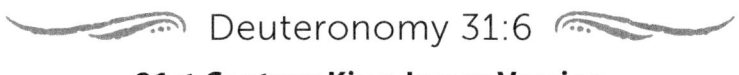 Deuteronomy 31:6

21st Century King James Version

6 Be strong and of good courage, fear not, nor be afraid of them; for the Lord thy God, He it is who doth go with thee. He will not fail thee nor forsake thee."

 Deuteronomy 31:6

New International Version

6 Be strong and courageous. Do not be afraid or terrified because of them, for the Lord your God goes with you; he will never leave you nor forsake you."

Question 18:

How do you fit God into the business of life? This is an example of how we did it.

[02/12/2022, 5:59:58 am] Andrea:

Thanks Dad. I just dropped Jack at swimming. He will get a taxi to the train station today because we don't want to have the bike with us later. Then train to school. At 2pm I will get on a train from Bristol that stops in Cheltenham where his school is and hopefully we have coordinated everything perfectly and Jack will get on there!

That's our day!

In-between all that we will be thinking about you and praying everything goes well.

Love you.

[02/12/2022, 6:42:09 am] Dad:

Thanks. That is hectic but God will see you through

We are at the hospital already. They open in1 hr. We carried my breakfast so I am eating.

Love you all

[02/12/2022, 6:43:48 am] Andrea:

What are you having?

[02/12/2022, 6:45:20 am] Dad:

Watermelon, apple pawpaw. Oats. Bread

[02/12/2022, 6:51:29 am] Andrea:

That sounds lovely! 😁

[02/12/2022, 7:07:28 am] Dad:

I read **Habakkuk 3 vs 17** last night and I was refreshed. You should read it at a time like this.

[02/12/2022, 7:15:01 am] Andrea:

I will read it this morning

[02/12/2022, 7:20:59 am] Dad:

Great

 Habakkuk 3:17-19

King James Version

17 Although the fig tree shall not blossom, neither shall fruit be in the vines; the labour of the olive shall fail, and the fields shall yield no meat; the flock shall be cut off from the fold, and there shall be no herd in the stalls:

18 Yet I will rejoice in the Lord, I will joy in the God of my salvation.

19 The Lord God is my strength, and he will make my feet like hinds' feet, and he will make me to walk upon mine high places. To the chief singer on my stringed instruments.

 Habakkuk 3:17-19

New International Version

17 Though the fig tree does not bud

and there are no grapes on the vines,

though the olive crop fails

and the fields produce no food,

though there are no sheep in the pen

and no cattle in the stalls,

18 yet I will rejoice in the Lord,

I will be joyful in God my Savior.

19 The Sovereign Lord is my strength;

he makes my feet like the feet of a deer,

he enables me to tread on the heights.

Andrea:

I don't really understand it. What does it mean.

Dad:

Our God is faithful and our God is gracious.

Question 19:

Dad what has been your biggest learning as you have battled cancer these last few years?

In 2019 Bola was diagnosed with prostate cancer. The challenges this raised were huge:

- Accessibility to good healthcare in Nigeria
- The cost having a surgery in the UK
- Cost of the drugs needed which were in excess of £1,000 a month
- Ability for my Dad at 78 and his wife 68 to manage the logistics of getting to hospitals
- Dealing with the trials of Nigerian living from lack of fuel to a sudden inability to withdraw money from your own bank account
- Knowing how harsh cancer treatment can be would Bola be able to withstand the effects

Despite of all this

- The surgery happened
- The drugs needed were purchased
- Bola overcame every side effect

Andrea:

I am so inspired by and proud of your mental and physical strength.

How did you cope with it?

What advice do you have for others?

What scripture was your greatest comfort?

How can family and friends help?

How has the experience affected your views on life?

Dad:

I had complained to my GP about frequent urination 2 years ago. I had a PSA result of 16. Normal range is 4.

I reckon that it was not given the appropriate attention. Funds were also not available to pursue and prosecute a follow up treatment.

It was late in 2021 when it had become very aggressive that succour was provided by my children and family.

I had a successful surgery in Manchester but unfortunately the cancer re occurred a year after.

I have been in and out of the hospital for tests, chemo and bone therapy since then.

Men over 40 years old pay special attention to Prostate issues. Treatment is simplified if detected early. My favourite scripture during this time has been Psalms 118 v17.

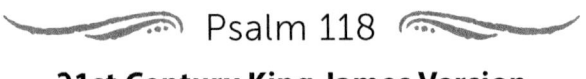 Psalm 118

21st Century King James Version

118 O give thanks unto the Lord, for He is good, for His mercy endureth for ever!

2 Let Israel now say that His mercy endureth for ever.

3 Let the house of Aaron now say that His mercy endureth for ever.

4 Let them that fear the Lord now say that His mercy endureth for ever.

5 I called upon the Lord in distress; the Lord answered me, and set me in an ample place.

6 The Lord is on my side; I will not fear. What can man do unto me?

7 The Lord taketh my part among them that help me; therefore shall I see what I desire upon them that hate me.

8 It is better to trust in the Lord than to put confidence in man.

9 It is better to trust in the Lord than to put confidence in princes.

10 All the nations compassed me about, but in the name of the Lord will I destroy them.

11 They compassed me about, yea, they compassed me about; but in the

name of the Lord I will destroy them.

12 They compassed me about like bees, they are quenched as the fire of thorns; for in the name of the Lord I will destroy them.

13 Thou hast thrust sorely at me that I might fall, but the Lord helped me.

14 The Lord is my strength and song, and has become my salvation.

15 The voice of rejoicing and salvation is in the tabernacles of the righteous; the right hand of the Lord doeth valiantly.

16 The right hand of the Lord is exalted; the right hand of the Lord doeth valiantly.

17 I shall not die, but live and declare the works of the Lord.

18 The Lord hath chastened me sorely, but He hath not given me over unto death.

 Psalm 118

New International Version

Psalm 118

1 Give thanks to the Lord, for he is good;

his love endures forever.

2 Let Israel say:

"His love endures forever."

3 Let the house of Aaron say:

"His love endures forever."

4 Let those who fear the Lord say:

"His love endures forever."

5 When hard pressed, I cried to the Lord;

he brought me into a spacious place.

6 The Lord is with me; I will not be afraid.

What can mere mortals do to me?

7 The Lord is with me; he is my helper.

I look in triumph on my enemies.

8 It is better to take refuge in the Lord

than to trust in humans.

9 It is better to take refuge in the Lord

than to trust in princes.

10 All the nations surrounded me,

but in the name of the Lord I cut them down.

11 They surrounded me on every side,

but in the name of the Lord I cut them down.

12 They swarmed around me like bees,

but they were consumed as quickly as burning thorns;

in the name of the Lord I cut them down.

13 I was pushed back and about to fall,

but the Lord helped me.

14 The Lord is my strength and my defence;

he has become my salvation.

15 Shouts of joy and victory

resound in the tents of the righteous:

"The Lord's right hand has done mighty things!

16 The Lord's right hand is lifted high;

the Lord's right hand has done mighty things!"

17 I will not die but live,

and will proclaim what the Lord has done.

Even when all human support fails and I am down to nothing, I will not deny God. I will rejoice in the Lord of my salvation.

Psalm 121

21st Century King James Version

121 I will lift up mine eyes unto the hills, from whence cometh my help!

2 My help cometh from the Lord, who made heaven and earth.

Psalm 121

New International Version

Psalm 121

A song of ascents.

1 I lift up my eyes to the mountains—

where does my help come from?

2 My help comes from the Lord,

the Maker of heaven and earth.

[07/01/2023, 10:12:17 am] Dad:

Can you imagine this is going to be my 5th chemo? Unbelievable how much resources had been consumed

I am grateful to you for contributions and support. I am almost there.

Even if I have no hair on my head I am surrounded by kind and caring people

[07/01/2023, 10:19:40 am] Andrea:

You still have hair.

[07/01/2023, 10:23:10 am] Andrea:

God still thinks you have a job to do or you wouldn't be here. Make all the efforts worth it by squeezing the most out of each day. Getting the most out of each day. Changing and influencing lives.

[07/01/2023, 10:30:22 am] Dad:

Very inspiring message. Thanks

[05/01/2023, 9:00:01 am] Dad:

The pains miraculously disappeared yesterday. Unbelievable. I am fine and eating well enough. I am taking my walk round. Just uplifted. Glory to God

[05/01/2023, 9:00:27 am] Andrea:

That's brilliant Dad!

[05/01/2023, 9:05:05 am] Dad:

I believe in miracles

[05/01/2023, 9:10:23 am] Dad:

I am still on the post chemo drugs that will end today. Then just iron and calcium tablets for the next Chemo 20th January

Thanks for the encouragement and support

God bless you

Keep On Believing

By Lucy Milward Booth, Mildred Duff

When you feel weakest, dangers surround,

Subtle temptations, troubles abound,

Nothing seems hopeful, nothing seems glad.

All is despairing ; oftentimes sad.

Refrain:

Keep on believing, Jesus is near.

Keep on believing, there's nothing to fear ;

Keep on believing, this is the way :

Faith in the night as well as the day.

If all were easy, if all were bright.

Where would the cross be ? where would the fight ?

But in the hardness God gives to you

Chances of proving that you are true.

God is your wisdom, God is your might ;

God's ever near you, guiding the right ;

He understands you, knows all you need ;

Trusting in Him you'll surely succeed.

Let us press on, then ; never despair !

Live above feeling, victory's there ;

Jesus can keep us so near to Him,

That nevermore our faith shall grow dim.

Question 20:

Are some messages only meant for the faithful and why is that?

[08/01/2023, 4:40:57 am] Dad:

Good morning. Happy Sunday

[08/01/2023, 7:08:26 am] Dad:

Video of a preacher

[08/01/2023, 8:03:05 am] Andrea:

Good morning Dad

[08/01/2023, 8:04:19 am] Andrea:

That was a bit of a depressing a preach. I don't disagree with the message but if someone new to church listened to that they may never come back. There's nothing uplifting about it.

[08/01/2023, 8:18:56 am] Dad:

I love the enduring riches

[08/01/2023, 11:08:24 am] Dad:

Moreover daughter. Some messages are meant for the faithful only.

[08/01/2023, 11:12:38 am] Andrea:

I just found the tone of his voice and the delivery of message depressing to hear first thing in the morning.

[08/01/2023, 11:15:01 am] Dad:

OK Please brighten up. God speaks in diverse ways.

[08/01/2023, 12:14:25 pm] Andrea:

I'm bright. I'm sharing that I thought the video was depressing.

[08/01/2023, 12:14:49 pm] Andrea:

There are one million uplifting preachers on the internet.

[08/01/2023, 12:15:21 pm] Dad:

Correct

[04/01/2023, 6:40:31 am] Dad:

Our devotional song this morning is

In Christ alone, My hope is found

Good memories!

[04/01/2023, 7:28:27 am] Andrea:

I LOVE that song! That's uplifting!

[04/01/2023, 7:40:27 am] Dad:

I am singing it all day, I know you love it

Worship Song
Recommendation

In Christ Alone

Songwriters: Keith Getty / Stuart Townend

Lyrics:

In Christ alone my hope is found

He is my light, my strength, my song

This cornerstone, this solid ground

Firm through the fiercest drought and storm

What heights of love, what depths of peace

When fears are stilled, when strivings cease

My comforter, my all in all

Here in the love of Christ I stand

In Christ alone who took on flesh

Fullness of God in helpless babe

This gift of love and righteousness

Scorned by the ones He came to save

Till on that cross as Jesus died

The wrath of God was satisfied

For every sin on Him was laid

Here in the death of Christ I live

There in the ground His body lay

Light of the world by darkness slain

Then bursting forth in glorious day

Up from the grave He rose again

And as He stands in victory

Sin's curse has lost its grip on me

For I am His and He is mine

Bought with the precious blood of Christ

No guilt in life, no fear in death

This is the power of Christ in me

From life's first cry to final breath

Jesus commands my destiny

No power of hell, no scheme of man

Can ever pluck me from His hand

Till He returns or calls me home

Here in the power of Christ I'll stand

[15/01/2023, 2:02:59 pm] Andrea:

How was church?

[15/01/2023, 2:17:35 pm] Dad:

Church was glorious. Much dancing,

Usually agile a week to next Chemo! But I go by faith next week

[15/01/2023, 2:19:31 pm] Andrea:

That's amazing!

[15/01/2023, 2:19:39 pm] Andrea:

I'm so glad you got to go

[15/01/2023, 2:19:44 pm] Andrea:

What did they sing

[15/01/2023, 2:21:56 pm] Dad:

The only song you may know is

[15/01/2023, 2:28:39 pm] Dad:

Others were short pentecostal choruses

Worship Song/Hymn Recommendation

Hold The Fort for I am coming

Hold the Fort

(P.P.Bliss)

Jesus signals still

Ho, my comrades! see the signal waving in the sky!

Reinforcements now appearing, victory is nigh.

Refrain

Hold the fort, for I am coming, Jesus signals still;

Wave the answer back to Heaven, By Thy grace we will.

See the mighty host advancing, Satan leading on;

Mighty ones around us falling, courage almost gone!

Refrain

See the glorious banner waving! Hear the trumpet blow!

In our leader's name we triumph over ev'ry foe.

Refrain

Fierce and long the battle rages, but our help is near;

Onward comes our great commander, cheer, my comrades, cheer!

Refrain

[15/01/2023, 2:26:48 pm] Andrea:

I like those

Question 21:

What to do when you disagree about when things should happen?

[16/03/2017, 12:37:31 pm] Andrea:

This is for your bus pass. Free travel on all buses when you are over 60! Bus stops just near us and you can visit church to your heart's content!!

[16/03/2017, 12:38:59 pm] Andrea:

Have a think about things outside church that you would like to do. There are clubs for everything here! Gardening, tennis, skydiving!!

[16/03/2017, 1:13:52 pm] Dad:

I would have loved some tennis if health allows. I have not played for a while. Do you reckon I come with a racket and tennis shoes in case the pains suddenly disappear?

[16/03/2017, 1:15:14 pm] Andrea:

Yes!!

[16/03/2017, 1:28:14 pm] Andrea:

I've contacted the chairman of Gainsborough Town Tennis Club. He said they would love to have you!!

[16/03/2017, 1:31:25 pm] Andrea:

I think you may have forgotten what your crazy daughter is like!! We don't sit still around here! You taught me to always have a program! Church is waiting for you to arrive and have jobs for you! We have a one week Christian Festival in summer with preachers from around the world, we are booked on that! And now tennis! You will rest and relax and be loved every second but you will NOT be bored!!

[16/03/2017, 1:45:00 pm] Dad:

I appreciate all these. Read **Ecclesiastes 3;1**. To every thing there is a season and a time for everything under the heavens. You should be familiar with that scripture! If not I will remind you

[16/03/2017, 1:51:13 pm] Andrea:

I am familiar with that scripture and the time is NOW! 😁 😁

# Ecclesiastes 3

21st Century King James Version

3 To every thing there is a season, and a time for every purpose under the heaven:

2 a time to be born, and a time to die; a time to plant, and a time to pluck up that which is planted;

3 a time to kill, and a time to heal; a time to break down, and a time to build up;

4 a time to weep, and a time to laugh; a time to mourn, and a time to dance;

5 a time to cast away stones, and a time to gather stones together; a time to embrace, and a time to refrain from embracing;

6 a time to get, and a time to lose; a time to keep, and a time to cast away;

7 a time to rend, and a time to sew; a time to keep silence, and a time to speak;

8 a time to love, and a time to hate; a time of war, and a time of peace.

New International Version

A Time for Everything

3 There is a time for everything,

and a season for every activity under the heavens:

2 a time to be born and a time to die,

a time to plant and a time to uproot,

3 a time to kill and a time to heal,

a time to tear down and a time to build,

4 a time to weep and a time to laugh,

a time to mourn and a time to dance,

5 a time to scatter stones and a time to gather them,

a time to embrace and a time to refrain from embracing,

6 a time to search and a time to give up,

a time to keep and a time to throw away,

7 a time to tear and a time to mend,

a time to be silent and a time to speak,

8 a time to love and a time to hate,

a time for war and a time for peace.

Question 22:

Dad what do you think about people who give and then spend the rest of the time complaining about how much they gave? If it is going to be difficult for you to give should you not give even though that would make you feel guilty?

[21/01/2017, 9:13:38 am] Dad:

In **2 Corinthians 9:7** God loves a cheerful giver.

[30/01/2017, 2:22:04 pm] Dad:

Hi daughter. Thanks a lot for all the assistance. They Will surely open the flood gates of abundance to You spiritually,materially,physically, émotionally and mentally IJN.

 2 Corinthians 9:7

21st Century King James Version

7 As every man purposeth in his heart, so let him give, not grudgingly or out of compulsion; for God loveth the cheerful giver.

 2 Corinthians 9:7

New International Version

7 Each of you should give what you have decided in your heart to give, not reluctantly or under compulsion, for God loves a cheerful giver.

Dad:

Giving to God is a financial covenant between God and the giver. **Luke 6 v 38**

 Luke 6:38

21st Century King James Version

38 Give, and it shall be given unto you: good measure, pressed down and shaken together and running over, shall men give into your bosom. For with the same measure that ye mete, therewith it shall be measured to you again."

 Luke 6:38

New International Version

38 Give, and it will be given to you. A good measure, pressed down, shaken together and running over, will be poured into your lap. For with the measure you use, it will be measured to you."

Question 23:

What does a Dad's prayer on his daughters birthday look like?

[01/03/2017, 10:10:10 am] Dad:

Thanks Jack and India for your Prayers. I am saying a loud Amen. God bless. Love you.

[02/03/2017, 12:48:18 pm] Dad:

Hi daughter,as You draw near your Birthday, God Will renew your youth like the Eagle. As your âgé Is , so shall your strength. 7th is round the corner. God's grâce Will get You there and far Beyond IJN

[02/03/2017, 1:01:52 pm] Andrea:

Thanks for thinking of me Dad.xx

[06/03/2017, 2:32:33 pm] Dad:

Hi daughter. (If The Lord will....) is biblical and that is what we preach. James 4: 13 to 15. Please read it. All is well. Iam packing and putting a few things in order.Love

 James 4:13-15
21st Century King James Version

13 Come now, ye that say, "Today or tomorrow we will go into such and such a city and continue there a year, and buy and sell and get gain";

14 whereas ye know not what shall be on the morrow. For what is your life? It is even a vapor that appeareth for a little time, and then vanisheth away.

15 Instead ye ought to say, "If the Lord will, we shall live and do this or that."

New International Version

Boasting About Tomorrow

13 Now listen, you who say, "Today or tomorrow we will go to this or that city, spend a year there, carry on business and make money." 14 Why, you do not even know what will happen tomorrow. What is your life? You are a mist that appears for a little while and then vanishes. 15 Instead, you ought to say, "If it is the Lord's will, we will live and do this or that."

[07/03/2017, 5:34:11 am] Dad:

Happy birthday. The Lord bless you and keep you. May He make his face to shine on you and be gracious to you, may He lift up His countenance of peace upon. He will satisfy you with long life and good health and prosperity. You will see your grandchildren IJN. I will call if The Lord will. Have a great day. Love. Dad

[07/03/2017, 4:07:48 pm] Dad:

Hi daughter. Leaving for mid week service in 30 minutes. God bless

[07/03/2017, 4:13:12 pm] Andrea:

Thanks Dad. I got your ecard too. Saw your call but was on the phone with my boss. Hope you are having a nice day.

[07/03/2017, 4:33:42 pm] Dad:

Simply rejoicing with you and thanking God

Question 24:

How do you handle things you are nervous about?

[23/03/2017, 9:55:02 am] Andrea:

In 11 days you will be here!!

[23/03/2017, 10:04:00 am] Dad:

Hi daughter. Stop making me nervous.! Got up from eating 3 days ago with a terrible back pain. Thank God It Is almost gone. I am ready for the trip by God's grâce

[23/03/2017, 10:08:11 am] Andrea:

Lovely. It's good timing actually because the children break up for Easter holidays on 5th. Jack has a swimming camp the week after so he's away but will be nice to get you introduced to the children while they are on holidays and less rushing around.

[23/03/2017, 10:13:10 am] Dad:

That Is wonderful. I am sure all things will work out well IJN

[30/03/2017, 7:48:09 pm] Dad:

Missed voice call

[31/03/2017, 7:37:48 am] Dad:

Morning daughter. Saw your missed call of 10pm yesterday only this morning. I slept 8.30 pm . I called you 7.30 when I did not receive a reply to my whatsapp Hope you are all fine. God bless

[31/03/2017, 9:02:41 am] Dad:

The Lord has already strengthened me for the journey and the experience I trust God to make everything work out for our good. Just one or two things to sort and I am set by God's grace

[31/03/2017, 9:13:16 am] Andrea:

You will be fine. 9 hours or so and you will be here. I will be waiting right there at the airport and within 15 minutes we will be home.

[31/03/2017, 9:23:38 am] Dad:

Amen

[03/04/2017, 11:28:38 am] Dad:

Read **Psalm 126**. God asked me to tell you: That everything will be alright from now on... You're to be victorious and will achieve all your goals. Today, Jesus Christ visited your home. On his way out, he took all your problems with him.

[03/04/2017, 10:28:14 pm] Andrea:

Ok.

[04/04/2017, 6:41:15 am] Andrea:

Today is the day that the Lord has made! I will REJOICE and be glad in it!!!

Here we are!! Today is the day! Can you believe this is coming true? This is a testimony of our combined faith in our father. Sing and skip and be happy because you deserve this. Enjoy every moment of the adventure!

There is nothing greater than my love for our father closely followed by my love for you which has stood firm through the test of time.

Hurry up!! We are waiting!!

[04/04/2017, 7:39:43 am] Dad:

Glory. to God. I had breakfast. Ready

[04/04/2017, 8:02:56 am] Andrea:

Great!

[04/04/2017, 12:13:04 pm] Dad:

In Lagos already. Biodun picked me. I will eat rest for three hours then off to the airport. Thanks for everything

[04/04/2017, 12:14:07 pm] Andrea:

Are you coming to England??

[04/04/2017, 12:16:47 pm] Dad:

Where else?

[04/04/2017, 12:17:08 pm] Andrea:

Just checking!! 😌 😌 😌

Dad:

Being nervous is a function of fear. **2 Timothy 1: 17** - God has not given us the spirit of fear but of love, boldness and of a sound mind. I pray nervousness out with this scripture.

 2 Timothy 1

21st Century King James Version

17 but when he was in Rome, he sought me out very diligently and found me.

Question 25:

How to deal with the loss of a loved one.

Soon afterwards Dad's Pastor died unexpectedly.

[04/01/2018, 11:11:23 am] Dad:

My Pastor collapsed and died in Church Tuesday night. It has been a trying period for all of us.We are making all the arrangements for the burial

[04/01/2018, 11:11:40 am] Andrea:

Oh my goodness

[04/01/2018, 11:14:22 am] Andrea:

I'm reading a book I got at Hillsong Church about dealing with tragedy. Thank God for the years you knew him, for the intentions in his heart. Through this it has shown me not to be afraid of death and I am not. It reaffirms my faith and actually makes me see things clearer in some ways.

[04/01/2018, 11:16:32 am] Dad:

We are in his house comforting the family

[04/01/2018, 11:32:34 am] Andrea:

Lord Jesus, please help the Pastors family at this painful time.

Remind them that we believe in the valley when it is preached in the sunshine and now in this valley of sadness we still believe in the valley of the shadow of death. We lift our hands to bless the name of God who gives and takes away. Just as Pastor was dedicated to the Lord at his birth and through the actions of his life, we commit him to the Lord again now. We thank Jesus for the honour of being his wife, children, co workers and friends. We confess our faith in the resurrection of Jesus and we put our hope in him anew. At this difficult time keep pointing in the right direction (Proverbs 6:22) and let God's words lead us from the moment we sleep to the moment we awake.

Proverbs 6:22

21st Century King James Version

22 When thou goest, it shall lead thee; when thou sleepest, it shall keep thee; when thou awakest, it shall talk with thee.

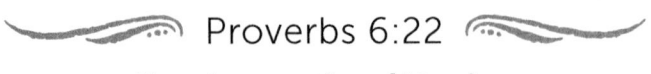
Proverbs 6:22

New International Version

22 When you walk, they will guide you;

when you sleep, they will watch over you;

when you awake, they will speak to you.

It is a privilege, not a right, to have the people we love in our lives. The apostle Peter said "you are a chosen generation, a royal priesthood, a holy nation, God's own special people that he brought out of darkness into His marvellous light" so you might proclaim his praises (**1 Peter 2:9**).

So never forget how incredible this man was and how God sees him. Amen.

[04/01/2018, 12:31:32 pm] Dad:

Amen. Thanks.God bless

1 Peter 2:9

21st Century King James Version

9 But ye are a chosen generation, a royal priesthood, a holy nation, a peculiar people, that ye should show forth the praises of Him who hath called you out of darkness into His marvelous light.

King James Version

9 But ye are a chosen generation, a royal priesthood, an holy nation, a peculiar people; that ye should shew forth the praises of him who hath called you out of darkness into his marvellous light;

Andrea:

I saw a post on Facebook that's how I knew. All these people are dying. Are you depressed?

Dad: Mon, 24 Jun 2019, 14:50

Depressed? No. It is an indication that the end is near. It teaches me to number my days so as to apply my heart to wisdom. Wisdom to live in love, light, worthy of the Lord. Wisdom to live according to His revealed characteristics. Wisdom to be loyal to Christ.

He had no friends. Most of his age mates had passed on.

My Motorola battery arrived Lagos last night. I will arrange to get it to Ibadan soon

Love you

Sent from Yahoo Mail for iPad

Andrea: Mon, 24 Jun 2019, 17:33

That's a great outlook. I read recently that death is a promotion.

Dad: Tue, 25 Jun 2019, 07:38

You are right Andrea. Death is a promotion but to only those who die in Christ. It is a promotion to a life in eternity where there is no more sorrow, death, disappointment, deceit, presence,hypocrisy, hatred,malice, hunger, thirst, or lack.

When we see Him, we will be like Him and be seen as we ought to be seen

Take care and remain blessed

Question 26:

How do you respond as a parent when your child makes a major life mistake?

I can only tell you how my Dad reacted to me and that when I had hit rock bottom his first, immediate and only reaction was to show me love.

Tue, 12 Mar 2019, 12:06

to me

Dear Andrea

It was with great joy that I received your letter today. I give God all the glory.

It is all in the glorious plan of The Almighty God for your life. There is a bright light at the end of the tunnel.

I agree it is a wilderness experience. Jesus came out of it in the power and strength of the Holy Spirit to do exploits

Please study the life of Daniel in the Bible and be assured that you will come out of it a better,stronger, and a more prosperous person.

Read **Psalm 121** also.

I love you anywhere, anyhow, anytime.

Hi Dad
I've been quite down lately I'm struggling with how overwhelming it feels to be 20 days away from coming home after so much. I have to get ready to face the shame and the re building. I was thinking about when you were moving to Ibadan and talked to me about how hard it felt to be starting again and yet you did. You have several times really.

I read psalm 121 "The Lord keeps you from all harm and watches over your life". I carry your email around with me and look at your words "I love you anywhere, anyhow, anytime" often.

I'm sorry I couldn't share more of this journey with you. I knew you would be too emotional about it. I felt like it could kill you and how could I live with that?

Thank you for your unconditional love which is such a comfort to me.

Have you moved house? The address looks different or perhaps I'm just used to seeing the P.O Box. How is your health? Any tennis?

Please come and visit. I need you.

Love Andrea

P.S- I'm reading Daniel.

God bless, Dad

 # Psalm 121

21st Century King James Version

121 I will lift up mine eyes unto the hills, from whence cometh my help!

2 My help cometh from the Lord, who made heaven and earth.

3 He will not permit thy foot to be moved; He that keepeth thee will not slumber.

4 Behold, He that keepeth Israel shall neither slumber nor sleep.

5 The Lord is thy keeper; the Lord is thy shade upon thy right hand.

6 The sun shall not smite thee by day, nor the moon by night.

7 The Lord shall preserve thee from all evil; He shall preserve thy soul.

8 The Lord shall preserve thy going out and thy coming in from this time forth, and even for evermore.

New International Version

Psalm 121

A song of ascents.

1 I lift up my eyes to the mountains—

where does my help come from?

2 My help comes from the Lord,

the Maker of heaven and earth.

3 He will not let your foot slip—

he who watches over you will not slumber;

4 indeed, he who watches over Israel

will neither slumber nor sleep.

5 The Lord watches over you—

the Lord is your shade at your right hand;

6 the sun will not harm you by day,

nor the moon by night.

7 The Lord will keep you from all harm—

he will watch over your life;

8 the Lord will watch over your coming and going

both now and forevermore.

Holy Spirit by Jesus Culture

Lyrics:

There's nothing worth more, that will ever come close

No thing can compare, You're our living hope

Your Presence

I've tasted and seen, of the sweetest of Loves

Where my heart becomes free, and my shame is undone

In Your Presence

Holy Spirit You are welcome here

Come flood this place and fill the atmosphere

Your Glory God is what our hearts long for

To be overcome by Your Presence Lord

Let us become more aware of Your Presence

Let us experience the Glory of Your Goodness

Holy Spirit You are welcome here

Come flood this place and fill the atmosphere

Your Glory God is what our hearts long for

To be overcome by Your Presence Lord

Question 27:

How did my Dad answer when I was in a very difficult situation that I was ashamed to talk about? This included job loss and a period of unemployment.

So there you have it. This is why I have been so distant and down.

Dad, you asked what you could pray for and this is it.

I just felt so isolated not being able to tell anyone and I know you understand the power of God. You don't have to respond immediately. I know it will be a shock.

[31/12/2017, 12:30:43 pm] Dad:

Just got back from Church. With God nothing shall be impossible. Remain blessed

[31/12/2017, 1:19:16 pm] Dad:

I kept thinking that all is not well. I kept praying general prayer. One needs to be specific with God on a matter like this.

Proverbs 21: 1 comes readily to mind. The heart of the king is in the Lord's hands and He twists to favour whosoever He will.The king is the authority handling the case. They will show you favour In Jesus Name. I had serious premonitions of impending problems but I narrowed them down to my health challenges. That was when I asked if there was anything amiss. I will never doubt you or deny God. Here the Church would rise in prayers and defence but it is different over there. I will write more later. Love you

 Proverbs 21

21st Century King James Version

21 The king's heart is in the hand of the Lord; as the rivers of water, He turneth it whithersoever He will.

2 Every way of a man is right in his own eyes, but the Lord pondereth the hearts.

3 To do justice and judgment is more acceptable to the Lord than sacrifice.

4 A haughty look and a proud heart, and the plowing of the wicked, are sin.

5 The thoughts of the diligent tend only to plenteousness, but of everyone that is hasty, only to want.

6 The getting of treasures by a lying tongue is a vanity which is tossed to and fro by them that seek death.

7 The robberies of the wicked shall destroy them, because they refuse to do judgment.

8 The way of man is froward and strange, but as for the pure, his work is right.

9 It is better to dwell in a corner of the housetop than with a brawling woman in a large house.

10 The soul of the wicked desireth evil; his neighbor findeth no favor in his eyes.

11 When the scorner is punished, the simple is made wise; and when the wise is instructed, he receiveth knowledge.

12 The righteous man wisely considereth the house of the wicked, how God overthroweth the wicked for their wickedness.

13 Whoso stoppeth his ears at the cry of the poor, he also shall himself cry, but shall not be heard.

14 A gift in secret pacifieth anger, and a bribe in the bosom, strong wrath.

15 It is a joy to the just to do judgment, but destruction shall come to the workers of iniquity.

16 The man that wandereth out of the way of understanding shall remain in the congregation of the dead.

17 He that loveth pleasure shall be a poor man; he that loveth wine and oil shall not be rich.

18 The wicked shall be a ransom for the righteous, and the transgressor for the upright.

19 It is better to dwell in the wilderness than with a contentious and angry woman.

20 There is treasure to be desired and oil in the dwelling of the wise, but a foolish man spendeth it up.

21 He that followeth after righteousness and mercy findeth life, righteousness and honor.

22 A wise man scaleth the city of the mighty, and casteth down the strength of their confidence.

23 Whoso guardeth his mouth and his tongue keepeth his soul from troubles.

24 Proud and haughty scorner is his name, who dealeth in proud wrath.

25 The desire of the slothful killeth him, for his hands refuse to labor;

26 he coveteth greedily all the day long, but the righteous giveth and spareth not.

27 The sacrifice of the wicked is an abomination; how much more so when he bringeth it with a wicked mind!

28 A false witness shall perish, but the man that heareth speaketh constantly.

29 A wicked man hardeneth his face, but as for the upright, he considereth his ways.

30 There is no wisdom, nor understanding, nor counsel against the Lord.

31 The horse is prepared for the day of battle, but safety is from the Lord.

 Proverbs 21

New International Version

21 In the Lord's hand the king's heart is a stream of water

that he channels toward all who please him.

2 A person may think their own ways are right,

but the Lord weighs the heart.

3 To do what is right and just

is more acceptable to the Lord than sacrifice.

4 Haughty eyes and a proud heart—

the unplowed field of the wicked—produce sin.

5 The plans of the diligent lead to profit

as surely as haste leads to poverty.

6 A fortune made by a lying tongue

is a fleeting vapor and a deadly snare.[a]

7 The violence of the wicked will drag them away,

for they refuse to do what is right.

8 The way of the guilty is devious,

but the conduct of the innocent is upright.

9 Better to live on a corner of the roof

than share a house with a quarrelsome wife.

10 The wicked crave evil;

their neighbors get no mercy from them.

11 When a mocker is punished, the simple gain wisdom;

by paying attention to the wise they get knowledge.

12 The Righteous One[b] takes note of the house of the wicked

and brings the wicked to ruin.

13 Whoever shuts their ears to the cry of the poor

will also cry out and not be answered.

14 A gift given in secret soothes anger,

and a bribe concealed in the cloak pacifies great wrath.

15 When justice is done, it brings joy to the righteous

but terror to evildoers.

16 Whoever strays from the path of prudence

comes to rest in the company of the dead.

17 Whoever loves pleasure will become poor;

whoever loves wine and olive oil will never be rich.

18 The wicked become a ransom for the righteous,

and the unfaithful for the upright.

19 Better to live in a desert

than with a quarrelsome and nagging wife.

20 The wise store up choice food and olive oil,

but fools gulp theirs down.

21 Whoever pursues righteousness and love

finds life, prosperity[c] and honor.

22 One who is wise can go up against the city of the mighty

and pull down the stronghold in which they trust.

23 Those who guard their mouths and their tongues

keep themselves from calamity.

24 The proud and arrogant person—"Mocker" is his name—

behaves with insolent fury.

25 The craving of a sluggard will be the death of him,

because his hands refuse to work.

26 All day long he craves for more,

but the righteous give without sparing.

27 The sacrifice of the wicked is detestable—

how much more so when brought with evil intent!

28 A false witness will perish,

but a careful listener will testify successfully.

29 The wicked put up a bold front,

but the upright give thought to their ways.

30 There is no wisdom, no insight, no plan

that can succeed against the Lord.

31 The horse is made ready for the day of battle,

but victory rests with the Lord.

Question 28:

As is sometimes the case with life, one blow was swiftly followed by another when my best friend died unexpectedly a few days later. How do you reset and start to recover from this?

[01/01/2018, 1:42:38 pm] Andrea:

I just heard she died on Saturday

[01/01/2018, 2:24:50 pm] Dad:

Very sad news. Perhaps best for her. God knows the ending from the beginning!

[01/01/2018, 2:25:16 pm] Dad:

Be comforted

[02/01/2018, 11:19:02 am] Dad:

Morning to you all. May God hear our prayers on the situation on ground In Jesus Name.. Will she be buried in London? May God grant her eternal rest. Just keep counting all your blessings and thank God for them.We should also confess all our wrong doings to God and ask for mercy. He will abundantly pardon. Have a peaceful day

[02/01/2018, 3:19:34 pm] Andrea:

I am heartbroken about her and will miss her terribly.

[13/01/2018, 7:41:42 am] Dad:

I always remember agreeing to walk her down the aisle on her wedding day!

[13/01/2018, 6:38:29 pm] Andrea:

Me too

Andrea:

Hi Dad

In church a few weeks ago they quoted something talking about how God wants us to have a great not ordinary life.

Dad:

If it that I have come that you may have life and have it more abundantly, it is **John 10 vs 10**

Love

Dad

 John 10:10

21st Century King James Version

10 The thief cometh not but to steal and to kill and to destroy. I am come that they might have life, and that they might have it more abundantly.

 John 10:10

New International Version

10 The thief comes only to steal and kill and destroy; I have come that they may have life, and have it to the full.

Question 29:

It's easy to be impatient with God expecting him to work on our timeline. How is it that God is always just on time?

In May 2023 it was disappointing to hear that the last round of chemo had not been as successful as we hoped. Another round was needed and possibly radiotherapy too. The cost of this was definitely a factor in our family.

The day my Dad got the news I also got the news of some money I had been hoping to get from a settlement.

Dad:

God is never late. Just at the time you need help he shows up. At the nick of time! May His Name be praised forever.

Andrea:

Amen. I thought the same thing. Just and perfectly in time!

Dad:

Read **Psalms 46:1**

 Psalm 46:1

21st Century King James Version

46 God is our refuge and strength, a very present help in trouble.

 Psalm 46

For the director of music. Of the Sons of Korah. According to alamoth.[b] A song.

1 God is our refuge and strength,

an ever-present help in trouble.

Andrea:

I like **Isaiah 58:11**

 Isaiah 58:11

21st Century King James Version

11 And the Lord shall guide thee continually, and satisfy thy soul in drought, and make fat thy bones; and thou shalt be like a watered garden, and like a spring of water whose waters fail not.

 Isaiah 58:11

New International Version

11 The Lord will guide you always;

he will satisfy your needs in a sun-scorched land

and will strengthen your frame.

You will be like a well-watered garden,

like a spring whose waters never fail.

Question 30:

Q: Parents make mistakes too. How do you deal with that as an adult child?

Over the years I have had a difficult relationship with my mum. Although they divorced many years ago my parents have remained friends. My Dad has often is the intermediary trying to defuse the latest disagreement.

Dad:

Please try and find time to study **Colossians 3 V23-24**

Colossians 3:23-24

21st Century King James Version

23 And whatsoever ye do, do it heartily, as to the Lord and not unto men,

24 knowing that from the Lord ye shall receive the reward of the inheritance, for ye serve the Lord Christ.

Colossians 3:23-25

New International Version

23 Whatever you do, work at it with all your heart, as working for the Lord, not for human masters, 24 since you know that you will receive an inheritance from the Lord as a reward. It is the Lord Christ you are serving. 25 Anyone who does wrong will be repaid for their wrongs, and there is no favouritism.

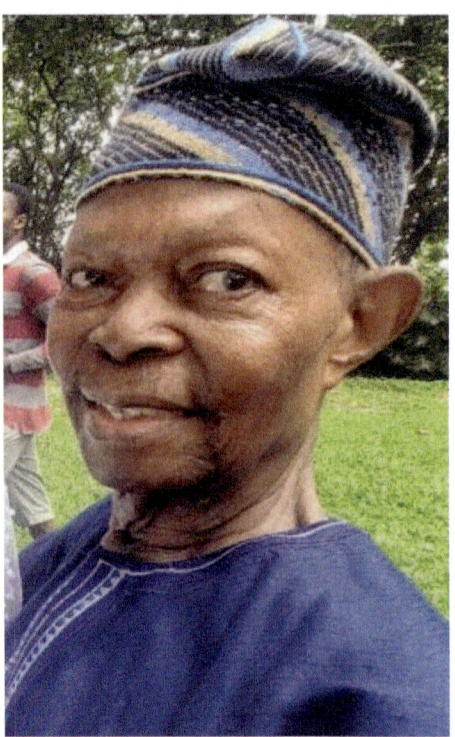

Question 31:

My two children are competitive swimmers. This brought with it many challenges over the years for them and I. My son was bullied and betrayed by someone he thought was a friend. For me expenses and logistics of coping as a single mum were huge factors.

Dad:

Good morning Daughter.

Where is the swimming on Sunday?

Andrea:

Bath University.

Dad:

It's a long drive. 1 hour to Bath and over 4 hours to Harrogate. Please rest well. God has done it before and He will do it again in Jesus Name.

Andrea:

Thanks Dad. This morning is another exam in Somerset. It's a lot for him and he's tired so I need to make sure I'm looking after him mentally. Very challenging time.

Dad:

Mind set. Determination. Experience. He will. He can. Blessedness!

In **Psalm 126 v 5** "that he who sows in tears will come back home rejoicing". Jack is sowing now with lots of difficulties but only for a while. The seeds will germinate and bring us all a bountiful harvest!

# Psalm 126

21st Century King James Version

126 When the Lord returned the captives to Zion, we were like them that dream.

2 Then was our mouth filled with laughter, and our tongue with singing. Then said they among the heathen, "The Lord hath done great things for them."

3 The Lord hath done great things for us, whereof we are glad.

4 Turn back our captivity, O Lord, as the streams in the South.

5 They that sow in tears shall reap in joy.

6 He that goeth forth and weepeth, bearing precious seed, shall doubtless come again with rejoicing, bringing his sheaves with him.

New International Version

Psalm 126

A song of ascents.

1 When the Lord restored the fortunes of[a] Zion,

we were like those who dreamed.[b]

2 Our mouths were filled with laughter,

our tongues with songs of joy.

Then it was said among the nations,

"The Lord has done great things for them."

3 The Lord has done great things for us,

and we are filled with joy.

4 Restore our fortunes,[c] Lord,

like streams in the Negev.

5 Those who sow with tears

will reap with songs of joy.

6 Those who go out weeping,

carrying seed to sow,

will return with songs of joy,

carrying sheaves with them.

Question 32:

What will I do without you?

May 10th 2023:

Dad:

Unfortunately the PSA went up instead of down. We had to repeat the PSA from a different lab to confirm. I will have to continue with the chemo with the possibility of adding radiation to it.

We thank God for your journey mercy and the exam. How many questions were there? How did Bisto (our dog) cope? If you are tired, reply in the morning.

Good night, God bless you all.

Andrea:

What level was your PSA?

Dad:

380 sadly. It had gone down to 60 before the suspension of the chemo. Please don't worry about it.

Andrea:

I'm not worried. It's just information and part of the journey. Please don't be worried. You are doing the best you can to manage it.

Dad:

It was 4000 in October when we started Chemo. It will surely start to go by God's grace. Thanks for standing by me all the way.

Andrea:

Of course. All the way.

Dad:

Good and reliable companion.

Andrea:

Yes. In the words of a worship song "you have been my father and my friend".

Dad:

I am very proud to be just that.

Thanks

Andrea:

Thank you too. ❤️

I will always have you whispering in my ear. What would Dad say? What would Dad do?

Dad:

I love that and I love you.

Andrea:

I love you too.

 1 Corinthians 13

21st Century King James Version

13 Though I speak with the tongues of men and of angels, but have not charity, I am become as sounding brass or a tinkling cymbal.

2 And though I have the gift of prophecy, and understand all mysteries and all knowledge, and though I have all faith so that I could remove mountains, but have not charity, I am nothing.

3 And though I bestow all my goods to feed the poor, and though I give my body to be burned, but have not charity, it profiteth me nothing.

4 Charity suffereth long, and is kind; charity envieth not; charity vaunteth not itself, is not puffed up;

5 doth not behave itself unseemly, seeketh not her own, is not easily provoked, thinketh no evil;

6 rejoiceth not in iniquity, but rejoiceth in the truth;

7 beareth all things, believeth all things, hopeth all things, endureth all things.

8 Charity never faileth. But whether there be prophecies, they shall fail; whether there be tongues, they shall cease; whether there be knowledge, it shall vanish away.

9 For we know in part, and we prophesy in part.

10 But when that which is perfect is come, then that which is in part shall be done away.

11 When I was a child, I spoke as a child, I understood as a child, I thought as a child; but when I became a man, I put away childish things.

12 For now we see through a glass, darkly, but then face to face. Now I know in part; but then shall I know, even as also I am known.

13 And now abideth faith, hope, charity, these three; but the greatest of these is charity.

 1 Corinthians 13

New International Version

13 If I speak in the tongues[a] of men or of angels, but do not have love, I am only a resounding gong or a clanging cymbal. 2 If I have the gift of prophecy and can fathom all mysteries and all knowledge, and if I have a faith that can move mountains, but do not have love, I am nothing. 3 If I give all I possess to the poor and give over my body to hardship that I may boast,[b] but do not have love, I gain nothing.

4 Love is patient, love is kind. It does not envy, it does not boast, it is not proud. 5 It does not dishonor others, it is not self-seeking, it is not easily angered, it keeps no record of wrongs. 6 Love does not delight in evil but rejoices with the truth. 7 It always protects, always trusts, always hopes, always perseveres.

8 Love never fails. But where there are prophecies, they will cease; where there are tongues, they will be stilled; where there is knowledge, it will pass away. 9 For we know in part and we prophesy in part, 10 but when completeness comes, what is in part disappears. 11 When I was a child, I talked like a child, I thought like a child, I reasoned like a child. When I became a man, I put the ways of childhood behind me. 12 For now we see only a reflection as in a mirror; then we shall see face to face. Now I know in part; then I shall know fully, even as I am fully known.

13 And now these three remain: faith, hope and love. But the greatest of these is love.

Worship Song
Recommendation

Goodness of God

Song by Bethel Music

I love You, Lord

For Your mercy never fails me

All my days, I've been held in Your hands

From the moment that I wake up

Until I lay my head

Oh, I will sing of the goodness of God

And all my life You have been faithful

And all my life You have been so, so good

With every breath that I am able

Oh, I will sing of the goodness of God

I love Your voice

You have led me through the fire

In the darkest night

You are close like no other

I've known You as a Father

I've known You as a Friend

And I have lived in the goodness of God (yeah)

And all my life You have been faithful (oh)

And all my life You have been so, so good

With every breath that I am able

Oh, I will sing of the goodness of God (yeah)

'Cause Your goodness is running after

It's running after me

Your goodness is running after

It's running after me

With my life laid down

I'm surrendered now

I give You everything

'Cause Your goodness is running after

It's running after me (oh-oh)

'Cause Your goodness is running after

It's running after me

Your goodness is running after

It's running after me

With my life laid down

I'm surrendered now

I give You everything

'Cause Your goodness is running after

It keeps running after me

And all my life You have been faithful

And all my life You have been so, so good

With every breath that I am able

Oh, I'm gonna sing of the goodness of God

(I'm gonna sing, I'm gonna sing)

'Cause all my life You have been faithful

And all my life You have been so, so good

With every breath that I am able

Oh, I'm gonna sing of the goodness of God

Oh, I'm gonna sing of the goodness of God

Question 33:

Andrea:

I remember when I first told you that I wanted to leave my husband and get a divorce. I expected you to lecture me about staying and frown on the very idea of it as unchristian. Instead, you were completely non-judgemental, kind, and supportive. Why?

Dad:

When you hinted that you were going to get separated I wasn't surprised. I didn't like it but I wasn't surprised. Right from the onset I had seen a lot of contention in the relationship. You were completely in charge administratively, financially and emotionally. You were in charge. Such a relationship just can't work. I can remember when you were pregnant and I came to the hospital with you for a scan and there was arguing. So I prayed but he did terrible things to you. I can't be happy about that.

God says he is interested in the peace and harmony of his people. If you stay in a relationship where you are unhappy it will affect you and affect everyone else. God does not want you to suffer.

Andrea:

What would you say to people considering separation or divorce?

Dad:

They must be considering divorce because of abusive or non compatibility in the relationship.

If they can make amends it's best not to separate. If they can live together in peace, harmony, love and joy they should always try to make it work. I think the children should always be considered because it will definitely affect them.

God does not like divorce but he does not hate a divorcee. God refers to marital relationships as a "mystery". That it is tough. He's actually talking about the church and Christ but he uses the metaphor of a husband and his wife.

Read Ephesians 5 31 - 33

 Ephesians 5:31-33

21st Century King James Version

31 "For this cause shall a man leave his father and mother, and shall be joined unto his wife, and they two shall be one flesh."

32 This is a great mystery, but I speak concerning Christ and the church.

33 Nevertheless, let every one of you in particular so love his wife even as himself, and the wife see that she reverence her husband.

 Ephesians 5:31-33

New International Version

31 "For this reason a man will leave his father and mother and be united to his wife, and the two will become one flesh."[a] 32 This is a profound mystery—but I am talking about Christ and the church. 33 However, each one of you also must love his wife as he loves himself, and the wife must respect her husband.

Question 34:

Andrea:

Growing up many of our family friends were Muslim. What would you have said if one day I told you I wanted to convert to Islam?

Dad:

That's a tough question. I have been brought up in a Christian faith and I brought you up in a Christian faith.

2 Corinthians 6 18 - We should not be unequally yoked together with unbelievers. So if I have brought you up as a Christian and you now tell me that you want to move away. **Hebrews 10: 26**. Having known the way of the Lord and you are now going back there is no more sacrifice for forgiveness. You accepted Jesus and all of a sudden you decide to change, that there is no forgiveness.

Andrea:

That's difficult. Does God still love them?

Dad:

Yes. God came to save the entire world including non believers but your salvation comes only from you believing in Jesus Christ. **John 3:16** Whoever believes in him will have everlasting life.

Having said that, if after I have explained all that to you you still want to convert you are still my child. Some of my half sisters converted to Islam because they married muslims and we celebrate Christmas together and Ramandan together!

Andrea:

What do you think about those that would banish people that do that and fall out with them forever?

Dad:

They don't know God. Very simple.

# 2 Corinthians 6:14-16

21st Century King James Version

14 Be ye not unequally yoked together with unbelievers, for what fellowship hath righteousness with unrighteousness? And what communion hath light with darkness?

15 And what concord hath Christ with Belial? Or what part hath he that believeth with an infidel?

16 And what agreement hath the temple of God with idols? For ye are the temple of the living God. As God hath said: "I will dwell in them and walk in them; and I will be their God, and they shall be My people."

# 2 Corinthians 6:14-16

New International Version

Warning Against Idolatry

14 Do not be yoked together with unbelievers. For what do righteousness and wickedness have in common? Or what fellowship can light have with darkness? 15 What harmony is there between Christ and Belial[a]? Or what does a believer have in common with an unbeliever? 16 What agreement is there between the temple of God and idols? For we are the temple of the living God. As God has said:

"I will live with them

and walk among them,

and I will be their God,

and they will be my people."

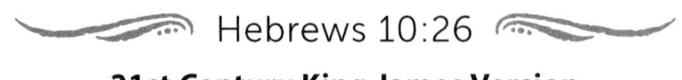# Hebrews 10:26

21st Century King James Version

26 For if we sin willfully after having received the knowledge of the truth, there remaineth no more sacrifice for sins,

Hebrews 10:26

New International Version

26 If we deliberately keep on sinning after we have received the knowledge of the truth, no sacrifice for sins is left.

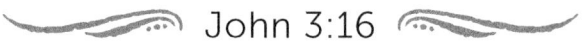

John 3:16

21st Century King James Version

16 "For God so loved the world that He gave His only begotten Son, that whosoever believeth in Him should not perish, but have everlasting life.

John 3:16

New International Version

16 For God so loved the world that he gave his one and only Son, that whoever believes in him shall not perish but have eternal life.

Worship Song Recommendation

There shall be showers of blessings

By Author: D. W. Whittle (1883)

Play "There shall be sh…"

on Amazon Music Unlimited (ad)

There shall be showers of blessing:

This is the promise of love;
There shall be seasons refreshing,
Sent from the Savior above.

Showers of blessing,
Showers of blessing we need;
Mercy-drops round us are falling,
But for the showers we plead.

There shall be showers of blessing-
Precious reviving again;
Over the hills and the valleys,
Sound of abundance of rain.

There shall be showers of blessing;
Send them upon us, O Lord!
Grant to us now a refreshing;
Come, and now honor Thy Word.

There shall be showers of blessing;
O that today they might fall,
Now as to God we're confessing,
Now as on Jesus we call!

There shall be showers of blessing,
If we but trust and obey;
There shall be seasons refreshing,
If we let God have His way.

Question 35:

Some people think the Old Testament should be largely ignored as this is strongly based on the old fashioned way of life at the time. That we should only use the new Testament. What do you think about that?

Dad:

The Bible is given by the inspiration of God. It teaches us the way to live. It's profitable for instruction, doctrine and perfection. In the Book of revelation he places a cross on whosoever takes out of the bible or whosoever adds to it.

Andrea:

So your view is that you can't just disregard the old testament and pick the parts of the new testament that you like.

Dad:

Yep. That is it.

 2 Timothy 3:16-17

21st Century King James Version

16 All Scripture is given by inspiration of God and is profitable for doctrine, for reproof, for correction, for instruction in righteousness,

17 that the man of God may be perfect, thoroughly equipped for all good works.

 2 Timothy 3:16-17

New International Version

16 All Scripture is God-breathed and is useful for teaching, rebuking, correcting and training in righteousness, 17 so that the servant of God[a] may be thoroughly equipped for every good work.

Blessed Assurance

Song by Alan Jackson

Blessed assurance, Jesus is mine!

Oh, what a foretaste of glory divine!

Heir of salvation, purchase of God

Born of his Spirit, washed in His blood

This is my story, this is my song

Praising my Savior all the day long

This is my story, this is my song

Praising my Savior all the day long

Perfect submission, perfect delight

Visions of rapture now burst on my sight

Angels descending bring from above

Echoes of mercy, whispers of love

This is my story, this is my song

Praising my Savior all the day long

This is my story, this is my song

Praising my Savior all the day long

Praising my Savior all the day long

Question 36:

Andrea:

"An eye for an eye". Do you think people sometimes misinterpret that?

I believe that ungodly people sometimes apply it as a reciprocal justice.

It was in the Mosaic law.

Exodus 21 23-27

Leviticus 21 19 - 21

In **Matthew 5 38 39** Jesus countered it.

We as Christians are not under the law but under grace.

 Exodus 21:23-27

21st Century King James Version

23 And if any misfortune follow, then thou shalt give life for life,

24 eye for eye, tooth for tooth, hand for hand, foot for foot,

25 burning for burning, wound for wound, stripe for stripe.

26 "And if a man smite the eye of his servant or the eye of his maid, that it perish, he shall let him go free for his eye's sake.

27 And if he smite out his manservant's tooth or his maidservant's tooth, he shall let him go free for his tooth's sake,

 Exodus 21:23-27

New International Version

23 But if there is serious injury, you are to take life for life, 24 eye for eye, tooth for tooth, hand for hand, foot for foot, 25 burn for burn, wound for wound, bruise for bruise.

26 "An owner who hits a male or female slave in the eye and destroys it must let the slave go free to compensate for the eye. 27 And an owner who knocks out the tooth of a male or female slave must let the slave go free to compensate for the tooth.

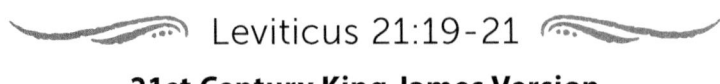 Leviticus 21:19-21

21st Century King James Version

19 or a man who is brokenfooted, or brokenhanded,

20 or crookbacked, or a dwarf, or who hath a blemish in his eye, or hath scurvy, or scabbed, or hath his stones broken—

21 No man that hath a blemish of the seed of Aaron the priest shall come nigh to offer the offerings of the Lord made by fire. He hath a blemish: he shall not come nigh to offer the bread of his God.

 Leviticus 21:19-21

New International Version

19 no man with a crippled foot or hand, 20 or who is a hunchback or a dwarf, or who has any eye defect, or who has festering or running sores or damaged testicles. 21 No descendant of Aaron the priest who has any defect is to come near to present the food offerings to the Lord. He has a defect; he must not come near to offer the food of his God.

 Matthew 5:38-39

21st Century King James Version

38 "Ye have heard that it hath been said, 'An eye for an eye, and a tooth for a tooth.'

39 But I say unto you that ye resist not evil, but whosoever shall smite thee on thy right cheek, turn to him the other also.

 Matthew 5:38-39

New International Version

Eye for Eye

38 "You have heard that it was said, 'Eye for eye, and tooth for tooth.'

39 But I tell you, do not resist an evil person. If anyone slaps you on the right cheek, turn to them the other cheek also.

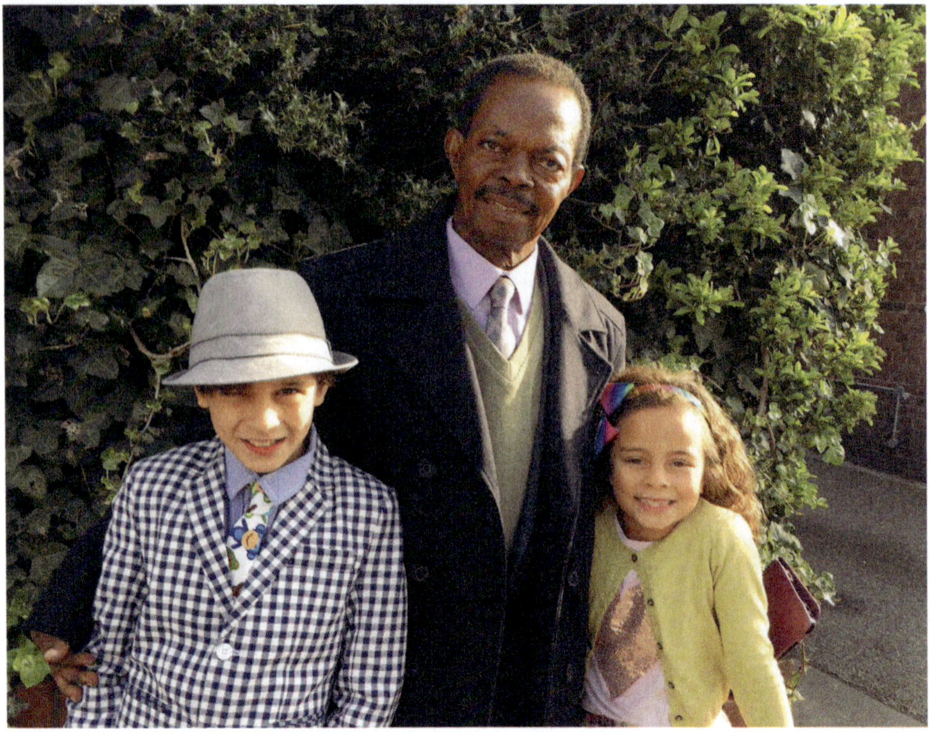

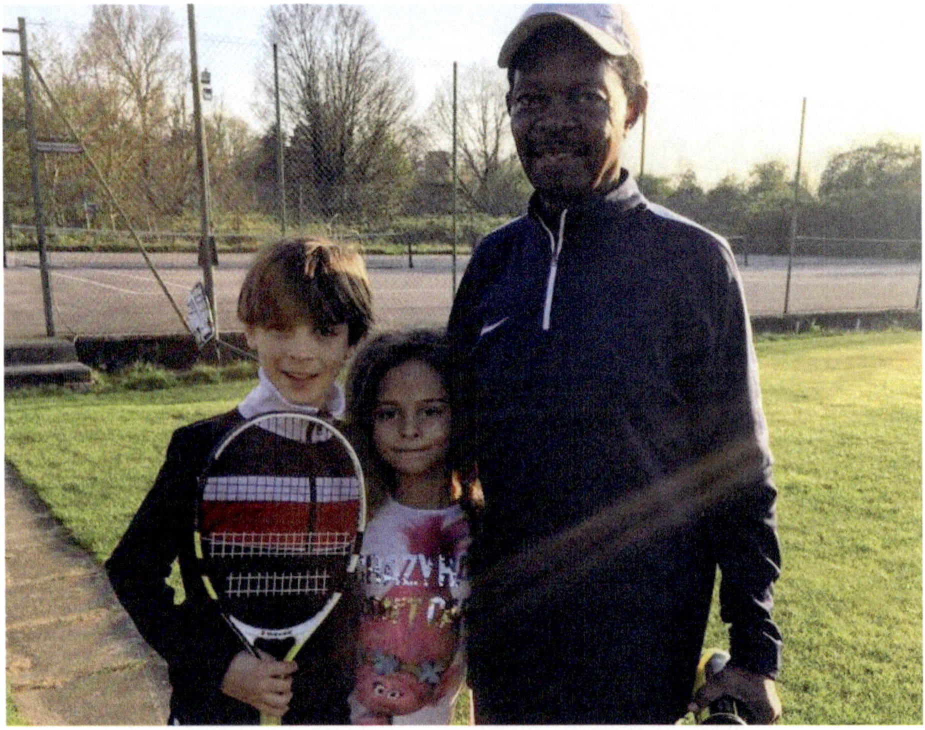

Question 37:

[31/01/2023, 5:39:04 am] Andrea:

We live in a culture where people hide their bad bits and social media is packed with good news, celebrations, high fives and likes.

Some of the most powerful things that happen to us in life are also deeply private. **Do you think it's important for people to share testimonials even though they may be revealing things that are deeply private and might cause embarrassment to the family?**

[31/01/2023, 7:10:03 am] Dad:

We can.

Testimonies are to glorify God and draw souls to His Kingdom.

Testimonies are supposed to be short and specific not detailed and revealing.

I was sick now I am healed.

I was blind now I see.

Read **John 9 25**

Andrea:

Personally I like the detail. If someone told me "I was blind now I see", I would say "Really, that's amazing, how did that happen"? I would want the details!

 John 9:25

21st Century King James Version

25 He answered and said, "Whether he be a sinner or not, I know not. One thing I know, that whereas I was blind, now I see."

 John 9:25

New International Version

25 He replied, "Whether he is a sinner or not, I don't know. One thing I do know. I was blind but now I see!"

Worship Song
Recommendation

Immortal Invisible God Only Wise

Words by Walter Chalmers Smith, usually sung to the tune, "St. Denio", originally a Welsh ballad tune.

1 Immortal, invisible, God only wise,

in light inaccessible hid from our eyes,

most blessed, most glorious, the Ancient of Days,

Almighty, victorious, Thy great name we praise.

2 Unresting, unhasting, and silent as light,

nor wanting, nor wasting, Thou rulest in might;

Thy justice, like mountains, high soaring above

Thy clouds, which are fountains of goodness and love.

3 To all, life Thou givest, to both great and small,

in all life Thou livest, the true life of all;

we blossom and flourish as leaves on the tree,

and wither and perish, but naught changeth Thee.

4 Great Father of glory, pure Father of light,

Thine angels adore Thee, all veiling their sight;

all praise we would render, O help us to see

'tis only the splendor of light hideth Thee!

Question 38:

Andrea:

One of my favourite passages is Joshua 1:9. This reminds me that everything will be ok and that I am never alone. Do you have any time in your life you can share when you have leaned on that passage?

Dad:

Joshua 1v 9 is my favorite scripture.

About a year ago I was very sick 3am with serious bleeding condition.

As I was passing out and my wife struggling to get me to the hospital I remembered Joshua 1.9 and with courage I told her that I would return to the house and God did it.

[28/04/2023, 9:24:08 pm] Andrea:

We are in our apartment. We are sharing with another family from the old club. Swimming starts tomorrow. We have to be there at 8am.

[28/04/2023, 11:56:50 pm] Dad:

Please have a wonderful night rest

[29/04/2023, 6:24:57 am] Andrea:

Hi Dad. I've been awake for about an hour. I'm getting Jack up in 30 minutes. He will have slept for 9 hours which is great. I have breakfast ready. I am just helping him make notes for his English exam. There are 17 poems he's supposed to know about so it's quite a lot of content.

[29/04/2023, 6:26:00 am] Andrea:

I make these yellow notes with key points and quotes and then we practice them everywhere we go.

[29/04/2023, 7:31:22 am] Dad:

17 poems? A lot!

With God and determination, Nothing is impossible

[29/04/2023, 8:25:01 am] Andrea:

Exactly

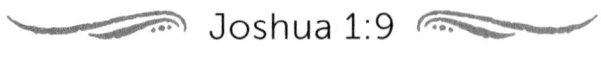

Joshua 1:9

21st Century King James Version

9 Have not I commanded thee? Be strong and of a good courage; be not afraid, neither be thou dismayed, for the Lord thy God is with thee whithersoever thou goest."

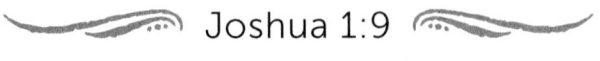

Joshua 1:9

New International Version

9 Have I not commanded you? Be strong and courageous. Do not be afraid; do not be discouraged, for the Lord your God will be with you wherever you go."

Worship Song
Recommendation

Yoruba/Englisd: Gbat'ab 'Oluwa Rin – Trust and Obey

'Gbat'ab 'Oluwa rin

N'nu 'mọlẹ ọrọ Rẹ;

Ọnà wa yíò ti mọlẹ to!

'Gbat'a ba nse 'fẹ Re,

On y'o ma ba wa gbe,

Ati awọn t'o gbẹkẹ wọn le.

Refrain

Sa gbękęle,
Ọna miran ko sí
Lati l'ayọ n'nu Jesu,
Ju pe, ka gbękęle.

Ko s'ohun to le dé,
L'oke tabi n'ilę,
To le ko agbára Rę l'oju;
Iyemeji, ęrú,
Ìbànúję, ękun
Ko le dúró, bi a gbękęle.

Refrain

Kò sí wàhálà mọ
Tabi ìbànúję,
O ti san gbogbo 'gbese wọnyi
Ko si aro kan mọ,
Tabi ifajuro,
Sugbọn 'bukun b'a ba gbękęle.

Refrain

A kò le f'ęnu sọ
Bi 'fę Rę ti pọ to

Titi ao fi f'ara wa rubọ;

Anu ti O nfi han

At'ayọ t'O nfun ni

Jẹ ti awọn ti o gbẹkẹle.

Refrain

Ni 'dapọ pẹlu Rẹ,

Ào joko l'ẹsẹ Rẹ,

Tabi ki a ma rin pẹlu Rẹ.

Awa yo gbọ Tirẹ,

Ào jisẹ t'O ran wa,

Ma bẹrù, sa gbẹkẹle nikan.

Amin.

English – Trust and Obey

Verse 1

When we walk with the Lord

In the light of His Word,

What a glory He sheds on our way;

While we do His good will,

He abides with us still,

And with all who will trust and obey.

Trust and obey,

For there's no other way

To be happy in Jesus,

But to trust and obey.

Verse 2

Not a shadow can rise,

Not a cloud in the skies,

But His smile quickly drives it away;

Not a doubt or a fear,

Not a sigh or a tear,

Can abide while we trust and obey.

Verse 3

Not a burden we bear,

Not a sorrow we share,

But our toil He doth richly repay;

Not a grief or a loss,

Not a frown or a cross,

But is blest if we trust and obey.

Verse 4

But we never can prove

The delights of His love,

Until all on the altar we lay;

For the favor He shows,

And the joy He bestows,

Are for them who will trust and obey.

Verse 5

Then in fellowship sweet

We will sit at His feet,

Or we'll walk by His side in the way;

What He says we will do;

Where He sends, we will go,

Never fear, only trust and obey.

Question 39:

Andrea:

Here is a scenario…A wife rudely answers her husband back in front of his friends. When they are gone he beats her, referencing the bible "honour your husband". Is he justified?

Dad:

No man is justified to beat the wife. **Ps 11v5**

Ephesians 4 32

Colossians 3 19

 Psalm 11:5

21st Century King James Version

5 The Lord trieth the righteous; but the wicked and him that loveth violence, His soul hateth.

 Psalm 11:5

New International Version

5 The Lord examines the righteous,

but the wicked, those who love violence,

he hates with a passion.

 Ephesians 4:32

21st Century King James Version

32 and be ye kind one to another, tenderhearted, forgiving one another, even as God for Christ's sake hath forgiven you.

# Ephesians 4:32

New International Version

32 Be kind and compassionate to one another, forgiving each other, just as in Christ God forgave you.

# Colossians 3:19

New International Version

19 Husbands, love your wives and do not be harsh with them.

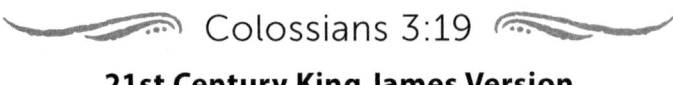# Colossians 3:19

21st Century King James Version

19 Husbands, love your wives and be not bitter against them.

When we walk with The LORD

By John H. Sammis 1887

When we walk with the Lord in the light of his Word

What a glory he sheds on our way!

While we do his good will, he abides with us still,

And with all who will trust and obey.

Trust and obey, for there's no other way

To be happy in Jesus, but to trust and obey.

Not a shadow can rise, not a cloud in the skies,

But his smile quickly drives it away;

Not a doubt or a fear, not a sigh nor a tear,

Can abide while we trust and obey.

Not a burden we bear, not a sorrow we share,

But our toil he doth richly repay;

Not a grief nor a loss, not a frown or a cross,

But is blest if we trust and obey.

But we never can prove the delights of his love

Until all on the altar we lay;

For the favor he shows, and the joy he bestows,

Are for them who will trust and obey.

Then in fellowship sweet we will sit at his feet,

Or we will walk by his side in the way;

What he says we will do, where he sends we will go,

Never fear, only trust and obey.

Andrea:

I think we should also have No woman no cry.

Dad:

Ahh! Bob Marley and the wailers!

Question 40:

Andrea:

Dad when you said this what did you mean?

[24/04/2019, 10:34:44 pm] Dad:

The truth about life is that everything in it and it has an expiry date.

Dad:

1 Peter 4v7 says that the end of everything is near so we should watch and pray

That is life. Only the word of God last forever everything else will expire

Good night

[24/04/2019, 11:11:55 pm] Andrea:

Night Daddy. Love you xx

 1 Peter 4-5

21st Century King James Version

4 For inasmuch then as Christ hath suffered for us in the flesh, arm yourselves likewise with the same mind, for he that hath suffered in the flesh hath ceased from sin,

2 that he no longer should live the rest of his time in the flesh to the lusts of men, but to the will of God.

3 For the time past of our life may suffice us to have wrought the will of the Gentiles, when we walked in lasciviousness, lusts, excess of wine, revelings, banquetings, and abominable idolatries;

4 wherein they think it strange that you run not with them to the same dissolute excess, speaking evil of you,

5 who shall give account to Him that is ready to judge the quick and the dead.

6 For, for this cause was the Gospel preached also to those who are dead, that they might be judged according to men in the flesh, but live according to God in the spirit.

7 But the end of all things is at hand: be ye therefore sober and watch unto prayer.

New International Version

Living for God

4 Therefore, since Christ suffered in his body, arm yourselves also with the same attitude, because whoever suffers in the body is done with sin. 2 As a result, they do not live the rest of their earthly lives for evil human desires, but rather for the will of God. 3 For you have spent enough time in the past doing what pagans choose to do—living in debauchery, lust, drunkenness, orgies, carousing and detestable idolatry. 4 They are surprised that you do not join them in their reckless, wild living, and they heap abuse on you. 5 But they will have to give account to him who is ready to judge the living and the dead. 6 For this is the reason the gospel was preached even to those who are now dead, so that they might be judged according to human standards in regard to the body, but live according to God in regard to the spirit.

7 The end of all things is near. Therefore be alert and of sober mind so that you may pray. 8 Above all, love each other deeply, because love covers over a multitude of sins. 9 Offer hospitality to one another without grumbling.

Question 41:

What does it mean when
He says we all have a job to do?

"Jesus came to earth because he had a job to do. We all have a job to do". He then read this exact same verse:

Jesus did not come to the world to set up an organization but to share a message

He needed people to work with him to share his message with the world

This is our work

We must do it while it is day The night cometh when no man can work

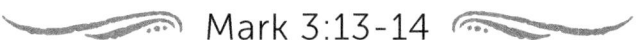 Mark 3:13-14

21st Century King James Version

13 And He went up onto a mountain, and called unto Him whom He would have, and they came unto Him.

14 And He ordained twelve, that they should be with Him, and that He might send them forth to preach,

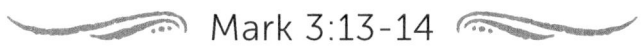 Mark 3:13-14

New International Version

Jesus Appoints the Twelve

13 Jesus went up on a mountainside and called to him those he wanted, and they came to him. 14 He appointed twelve[a] that they might be with him and that he might send them out to preach

Worship Song Recommendation

Praise The Lord The King of heaven

By Henry Francis Lyte, Alan Gray and John Goss

Praise, my soul, the King of heaven;

To his feet your tribute bring.

Ransomed, healed, restored, forgiven,

Evermore his praises sing.

Alleluia, alleluia!

Praise the everlasting King!

Praise him for his grace and favor

To his people in distress.

Praise him, still the same as ever,

Slow to chide, and swift to bless.

Alleluia, alleluia!

Glorious in his faithfulness!

Fatherlike he tends and spares us;

Well our feeble frame he knows.

In his hand he gently bears us,

Rescues us from all our foes.

Alleluia, alleluia!

Widely yet his mercy flows!

Angels, help us to adore him;

You behold him face to face.

Sun and moon, bow down before him,

Dwellers all in time and space.

Alleluia, alleluia!

Praise with us the God of grace!

Question 42:

What can I read Dad? I feel so much bitterness towards that friend who betrayed me.

Dad:

Please read **Genesis 37** about Joseph's story of betrayal.

 Genesis 37

21st Century King James Version

37 And Jacob dwelt in the land wherein his father was a stranger, in the land of Canaan.

2 These are the generations of Jacob. Joseph, being seventeen years old, was feeding the flock with his brethren; and the lad was with the sons of Bilhah, and with the sons of Zilpah, his father's wives. And Joseph brought unto his father an evil report about them.

3 Now Israel loved Joseph more than all his children, because he was the son of his old age; and he made him a coat of many colors.

4 And when his brethren saw that their father loved him more than all his brethren, they hated him and could not speak peaceably unto him.

5 And Joseph dreamed a dream, and he told it to his brethren; and they hated him yet the more.

6 And he said unto them, "Hear, I pray you, this dream which I have dreamed:

7 For, behold, we were binding sheaves in the field, and lo, my sheaf arose and also stood upright; and behold, your sheaves stood round about, and made obeisance to my sheaf."

8 And his brethren said to him, "Shalt thou indeed reign over us? Or shalt thou indeed have dominion over us?" And they hated him yet the more for his dreams and for his words.

9 And he dreamed yet another dream, and told it to his brethren and said, "Behold, I have dreamed one dream more; and behold, the sun and the moon and the eleven stars made obeisance to me."

10 And he told it to his father and to his brethren; and his father rebuked him and said unto him, "What is this dream that thou hast dreamed? Shall I and thy mother and thy brethren indeed come to bow down ourselves to thee to the earth?"

11 And his brethren envied him, but his father observed the saying.

12 And his brethren went to feed their father's flock in Shechem.

13 And Israel said unto Joseph, "Do not thy brethren feed the flock in Shechem? Come, and I will send thee unto them." And he said to him, "Here am I."

14 And he said to him, "Go, I pray thee, see whether it be well with thy brethren and well with the flocks, and bring me word again." So he sent him out of the Vale of Hebron, and he came to Shechem.

15 And a certain man found him, and behold, he was wandering in the field; and the man asked him, saying, "What seekest thou?"

16 And he said, "I seek my brethren. Tell me, I pray thee, where they feed their flocks."

17 And the man said, "They have departed hence, for I heard them say, 'Let us go to Dothan.'" And Joseph went after his brethren, and found them in Dothan.

18 And when they saw him afar off, even before he came near unto them, they conspired against him to slay him.

19 And they said one to another, "Behold, this dreamer cometh.

20 Come now therefore and let us slay him, and cast him into some pit, and we will say, 'Some evil beast hath devoured him'; and we shall see what will become of his dreams."

21 And Reuben heard it, and he delivered him out of their hands and said, "Let us not kill him."

22 And Reuben said unto them, "Shed no blood, but cast him into this pit that is in the wilderness, and lay no hand upon him" — that he might rid him out of their hands to deliver him to his father again.

23 And it came to pass, when Joseph had come unto his brethren, that they stripped Joseph of his coat, his coat of many colors that was on him;

24 and they took him and cast him into a pit. And the pit was empty; there was no water in it.

25 And they sat down to eat bread; and they lifted up their eyes and looked,

and behold, a company of Ishmaelites came from Gilead with their camels, bearing spices and balm and myrrh, going to carry them down to Egypt.

26 And Judah said unto his brethren, "What profit is it if we slay our brother and conceal his blood?

27 Come, and let us sell him to the Ishmaelites, and let not our hand be upon him; for he is our brother and our flesh." And his brethren were content.

28 Then there passed by Midianite merchantmen; and they drew and lifted up Joseph out of the pit, and sold Joseph to the Ishmaelites for twenty pieces of silver. And they brought Joseph into Egypt.

29 And Reuben returned unto the pit, and behold, Joseph was not in the pit; and he rent his clothes.

30 And he returned unto his brethren and said, "The child is no more; and I, whither shall I go?"

31 And they took Joseph's coat, and killed a kid from the goats, and dipped the coat in the blood.

32 And they sent the coat of many colors, and they brought it to their father and said, "This have we found. Know now whether it be thy son's coat or not?"

33 And he knew it, and said, "It is my son's coat. An evil beast hath devoured him. Joseph is without doubt rent in pieces."

34 And Jacob rent his clothes, and put sackcloth upon his loins, and mourned for his son many days.

35 And all his sons and all his daughters rose up to comfort him; but he refused to be comforted, and he said, "For I will go down into the grave unto my son, mourning." Thus his father wept for him.

36 And the Midianites sold him into Egypt unto Potiphar, an officer of Pharaoh's and captain of the guard.

New International Version

Joseph's Dreams

37 Jacob lived in the land where his father had stayed, the land of Canaan.

2 This is the account of Jacob's family line.

Joseph, a young man of seventeen, was tending the flocks with his brothers, the sons of Bilhah and the sons of Zilpah, his father's wives, and he brought their father a bad report about them.

3 Now Israel loved Joseph more than any of his other sons, because he had been born to him in his old age; and he made an ornate[a] robe for him. 4 When his brothers saw that their father loved him more than any of them, they hated him and could not speak a kind word to him.

5 Joseph had a dream, and when he told it to his brothers, they hated him all the more. 6 He said to them, "Listen to this dream I had: 7 We were binding sheaves of grain out in the field when suddenly my sheaf rose and stood upright, while your sheaves gathered around mine and bowed down to it."

8 His brothers said to him, "Do you intend to reign over us? Will you actually rule us?" And they hated him all the more because of his dream and what he had said.

9 Then he had another dream, and he told it to his brothers. "Listen," he said, "I had another dream, and this time the sun and moon and eleven stars were bowing down to me."

10 When he told his father as well as his brothers, his father rebuked him and said, "What is this dream you had? Will your mother and I and your brothers actually come and bow down to the ground before you?" 11 His brothers were jealous of him, but his father kept the matter in mind.

Joseph Sold by His Brothers

12 Now his brothers had gone to graze their father's flocks near Shechem, 13 and Israel said to Joseph, "As you know, your brothers are grazing the flocks near Shechem. Come, I am going to send you to them."

"Very well," he replied.

14 So he said to him, "Go and see if all is well with your brothers and with the flocks, and bring word back to me." Then he sent him off from the Valley of Hebron.

When Joseph arrived at Shechem, 15 a man found him wandering around in the fields and asked him, "What are you looking for?"

16 He replied, "I'm looking for my brothers. Can you tell me where they are grazing their flocks?"

17 "They have moved on from here," the man answered. "I heard them say, 'Let's go to Dothan.'"

So Joseph went after his brothers and found them near Dothan. 18 But they saw him in the distance, and before he reached them, they plotted to kill him.

19 "Here comes that dreamer!" they said to each other. 20 "Come now, let's kill him and throw him into one of these cisterns and say that a ferocious animal devoured him. Then we'll see what comes of his dreams."

21 When Reuben heard this, he tried to rescue him from their hands. "Let's not take his life," he said. 22 "Don't shed any blood. Throw him into this cistern here in the wilderness, but don't lay a hand on him." Reuben said this to rescue him from them and take him back to his father.

23 So when Joseph came to his brothers, they stripped him of his robe—the ornate robe he was wearing— 24 and they took him and threw him into the cistern. The cistern was empty; there was no water in it.

25 As they sat down to eat their meal, they looked up and saw a caravan of Ishmaelites coming from Gilead. Their camels were loaded with spices, balm and myrrh, and they were on their way to take them down to Egypt.

26 Judah said to his brothers, "What will we gain if we kill our brother and cover up his blood? 27 Come, let's sell him to the Ishmaelites and not lay our hands on him; after all, he is our brother, our own flesh and blood." His brothers agreed.

28 So when the Midianite merchants came by, his brothers pulled Joseph up out of the cistern and sold him for twenty shekels[b] of silver to the Ishmaelites, who took him to Egypt.

29 When Reuben returned to the cistern and saw that Joseph was not there, he tore his clothes. 30 He went back to his brothers and said, "The boy isn't there! Where can I turn now?"

31 Then they got Joseph's robe, slaughtered a goat and dipped the robe in the blood. 32 They took the ornate robe back to their father and said, "We found this. Examine it to see whether it is your son's robe."

33 He recognized it and said, "It is my son's robe! Some ferocious animal has devoured him. Joseph has surely been torn to pieces."

34 Then Jacob tore his clothes, put on sackcloth and mourned for his son many days. 35 All his sons and daughters came to comfort him, but he refused to be comforted. "No," he said, "I will continue to mourn until I join my son in the grave." So his father wept for him.

36 Meanwhile, the Midianites[c] sold Joseph in Egypt to Potiphar, one of Pharaoh's officials, the captain of the guard.

Also Matthew 10:35

Matthew 10:35

21st Century King James Version

35 For I am come to 'set a man at variance against his father, and the daughter against her mother, and the daughter-in-law against her mother-in-law.'

Matthew 10:35

New International Version

35 For I have come to turn

"'a man against his father,

a daughter against her mother,

a daughter-in-law against her mother-in-law—

[16/08/2019, 6:41:58 am] Andrea:

I don't know if I'm bitter towards her or just disappointed in who she revealed herself to be and angry at myself for trusting the wrong people.

[16/08/2019, 6:46:01 am] Dad:

I try to read **Psalm 121:1-8** regularly. It blesses my soul

[07/10/2019, 8:21:58 am] Dad:

Morning daughter. Yesterday was hectic. we are servants. I am blessed already to learn that serving is humility, caring, commitment, operating in the power of the holy spirit.

I will continue when I am back from my walk.

Thanks

God bless

Love you all

 Psalm 121

21st Century King James Version

121 I will lift up mine eyes unto the hills, from whence cometh my help!

2 My help cometh from the Lord, who made heaven and earth.

3 He will not permit thy foot to be moved; He that keepeth thee will not slumber.

4 Behold, He that keepeth Israel shall neither slumber nor sleep.

5 The Lord is thy keeper; the Lord is thy shade upon thy right hand.

6 The sun shall not smite thee by day, nor the moon by night.

7 The Lord shall preserve thee from all evil; He shall preserve thy soul.

8 The Lord shall preserve thy going out and thy coming in from this time forth, and even for evermore.

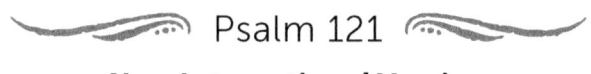 Psalm 121

New International Version

Psalm 121

A song of ascents.

1 I lift up my eyes to the mountains—

  where does my help come from?

2 My help comes from the Lord,

  the Maker of heaven and earth.

3 He will not let your foot slip—

   he who watches over you will not slumber;

4 indeed, he who watches over Israel

   will neither slumber nor sleep.

5 The Lord watches over you—

   the Lord is your shade at your right hand;

6 the sun will not harm you by day,

   nor the moon by night.

7 The Lord will keep you from all harm—

   he will watch over your life;

8 the Lord will watch over your coming and going

   both now and forevermore.

Question 43:

Everything belongs to God from our possessions, money to our talents. Where does it tell us that Dad?

[24/02/2017, 11:39:06 am] Andrea:

I don't want anything, thanks Dad.

I will ask them. They are currently outside with the horses.

[24/02/2017, 11:41:34 am] Dad:

Am I allowed to carry plantain or dodo Ikire like in the past?

02/06/2017, 9:44:31 pm] Dad:

How was your day? Thanks for introducing me to Premier Christian Radio. Good night. God bless

[31/03/2017, 7:52:08 am] Dad:

Hi daughter, how are you all doing? Are you still counting the days? Please go ahead and count. I can't be nervous anymore.! How is work going? Do you move round as in Storage Deluxe?

[31/03/2017, 7:53:47 am] Dad:

I forwarded it

[31/03/2017, 8:10:18 am] Andrea:

I've got it now!

[31/03/2017, 8:15:59 am] Andrea:

Yes! We are all counting and are so excited! I don't move around quite as much because then I didn't have children!!

Just relax and enjoy the whole experience. It is a gift to us from our father and he wants us to rejoice in it!!

I've been telling everyone "my Dad is coming"! So I am just finalising plans for Easter Sunday and our party! I washed your bedding and everything is ready for you now. Nothing left to do.

How are you feeling? I just dropped Jack at school after early morning swimming. I went to bed a bit late so I am quite tired.

This time next week you will be at home having just waved your granddaughter off to school. While you are here she won't need to get up at 4am to come with me when I take Jack. So that will be a big help and much better for her.

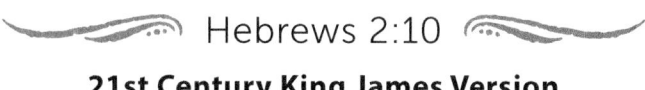

Hebrews 2:10

21st Century King James Version

10 For it became Him, for whom are all things, and by whom are all things, in bringing many sons unto glory, to make the Captain of their salvation perfect through sufferings.

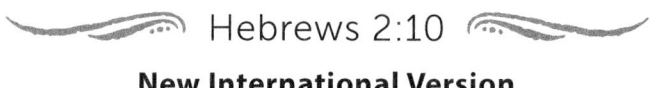

Hebrews 2:10

New International Version

10 In bringing many sons and daughters to glory, it was fitting that God, for whom and through whom everything exists, should make the pioneer of their salvation perfect through what he suffered.

Acts 17:28

21st Century King James Version

28 For in Him we live, and move, and have our being; as also certain of your own poets have said, 'For we are also His offspring.'

Acts 17:28

New International Version

28 'For in him we live and move and have our being.'[a] As some of your own poets have said, 'We are his offspring.'

Question 44:

Do you think people run to God in the bad times but sometimes forget to thank him in the good times?

Dad:

I agree that most of us run to God when life is tough. We refuse to give him thanks when we receive the blessings. This is the nature of man. God commands us to give him thanks in all things because this is the will of God for our lives.

 1 Thessalonians 5:18

21st Century King James Version

18 In every thing give thanks, for this is the will of God in Christ Jesus concerning you.

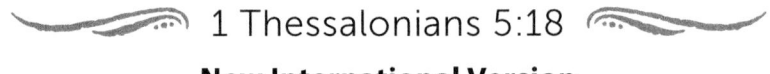 1 Thessalonians 5:18

New International Version

18 give thanks in all circumstances; for this is God's will for you in Christ Jesus.

In Luke the lepers were cleansed. Only one returned to give Jesus thanks. He was the only one that received his perfect healing.

[03/06/2017, 7:09:15 pm] Andrea:

The chickens were out all day long today. I just put them in so the dogs can come out. They are getting even friendlier. I went and picked one up to take back to the coop and the other two just followed me and went in by themselves!!

[03/06/2017, 7:12:51 pm] Dad:

They are becoming human! I love fried chicken

[03/06/2017, 7:36:47 pm] Andrea:

Noooo! Not these chickens!

[28/04/2019, 5:38:08 am] Dad:

Morning daughter

As you wake up this morning you will receive grace to do exploits for God In Jesus Name

You will not run into error. You will not run into danger. There will be no domestic accident in your domain In Jesus Name.

God will lead you and prosper your ways.

God bless you all.

[10/05/2019, 12:35:55 pm] Andrea:

Next... look at who we can help. Where in front of our nose is there a need for compassion. We all have a job to do in the name of Jesus.

Maybe your job is me!! You sow into me and then what I produce in terms of godly children and how I support and change the lives of others has a huge impact.

[10/05/2019, 1:54:47 pm] Dad:

This is God in action! We give Him all the glory.

Question 45:

Do you think that all of our life experiences are designed by God? From the music we listen to or the friends or jobs we have? That everything is already planned out?

Dad:

I believe that all of our life experiences are designed by God. Please consider the following scriptures

Revelations 22 13 I am the alpha and the Omega, the beginning and the ending.

Jeremiah 1:5 Before I formed you I knew you.

Psalms 139:13 Also confirms this.

But all for His purpose. He will not impose His will on us. He has set us the way of good and evil, He wants us to choose good.

 Jeremiah 1:5

21st Century King James Version

5 "Before I formed thee in the belly I knew thee, and before thou camest forth out of the womb I sanctified thee, and I ordained thee a prophet unto the nations."

 Jeremiah 1:5

New International Version

5 "Before I formed you in the womb I knew[a] you,

before you were born I set you apart;

I appointed you as a prophet to the nations."

Revelation 22:13

21st Century King James Version

13 I am Alpha and Omega, the Beginning and the End, the First and the Last."

Revelation 22:13

New International Version

13 I am the Alpha and the Omega, the First and the Last, the Beginning and the End.

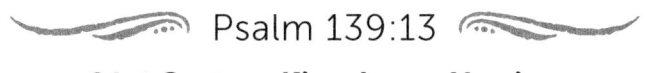

Psalm 139:13

21st Century King James Version

13 For Thou hast possessed my reins. Thou hast covered me in my mother's womb.

Andrea:

Sun, 31 May 2015, 23:37

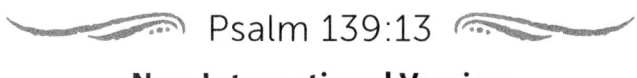

Psalm 139:13

New International Version

13 For you created my inmost being;

you knit me together in my mother's womb.

Hi Dad

Hope you are well.

I am watching a documentary on Motown which is so wonderful. You would absolutely love it. I wish I was watching it with you!

Who was your favourite artist and what were your favourite songs?

Dad: Wed, 3 Jun 2015, 19:23

to me

Hi daughter

Motown was my favourite record label and I loved all the artists. I actually met Jim Ruffin personally.

These were my favourites:

Mary Wells – My Guy

Smokey Robinson & The Miracles

Berry Gordy

Dionne Warwick

The Four Tops – Reach out and I'll be there – Levi Holland

Mary Wilson – Stop in the name of love

Otis Williams and Edwin Starr – War

You can't Hurry Love – The Supremes

Tears of a clown

Marvin Gaye and Timmi Terrell

Ashford & Simpson

Diana Ross – Aint no mountain high enough

Jimmy Ruffin – What becomes of the broken hearted

Gladys Knight & Marvin Gaye – Both did versions of I heard it through the grapevine

Love you.xx

Sat, 5 Apr 2014, 07:42

to Dad

Visiting the Holy Land

Hi Dad

Here are a few pictures from our trip so far.

Yesterday we spent the day in Jerusalem. It is an amazing place with Christians, Jews and Arabs all visiting, working, praying in complete harmony.

It is beautiful and helps you to really imagine the stories you have read. Some of the images we have in our minds are not accurate and you see that here. For example Jesus was not born in an outdoor stable the way it is commonly depicted. The buildings in Bethlehem were set into the rock. The front park coolest and the back part warmest. It is also unlikely that "no room at the inn" meant that all accommodation was full. More likely from a chat I had with a Christian historian that there was a stigma because Mary wasn't married and it was not appropriate for people to be seen to be accommodating such a woman. When they were given the stable this would be a room at the back where animals were often kept to keep them from the cold and it also would be more discrete that the homeowner had an up married pregnant woman at his place.

Bethlehem means house of bread because of the many farmers there growing wheat, which got made into bread. People travelling to Jerusalem would stop in Bethlehem as a pit stop to drink water and eat bread.

There are loads of interesting facts. Everywhere you go there are archaeologists and historians. One woman told me that before something is thought to be creditable such as how can they confirm this was the exact location of the tomb or the manger? They have to have three things: 1) a tradition - stories told by generations and passed down showing different unrelated people all verifying the same thing.

2) Historical confirmation - for example Jesus was born around April not December. They know this based on context. So shepherds would not have been in the fields in wintery December but would in spring for lambing season. Also the wise men saw a comet that is well documented. This was the star that would point them to Bethlehem, but it would take them about 3 months to arrive there so unlikely that both shepherds and wise men visited baby Jesus on the same night.

I think what is so obvious once you're here is that there is no question at all that a man named Jesus walked these streets. We believe it because of faith but there is massive tangible evidence to support the things we read all preserved here. Whether people believe Jesus was the son of a God or not is the debate of the three religions, but no one can come here and leave with any doubt that he existed.

The pictures show these things:

Outside and then inside the place of the crucifixion

Wailing wall

Gethsemane

Bethlehem and the star that marks the birthplace of Christ.

View of the church of the nativity which was built around the caves where Jesus was born to protect the site. It is the oldest church in the world at 1700 years old.

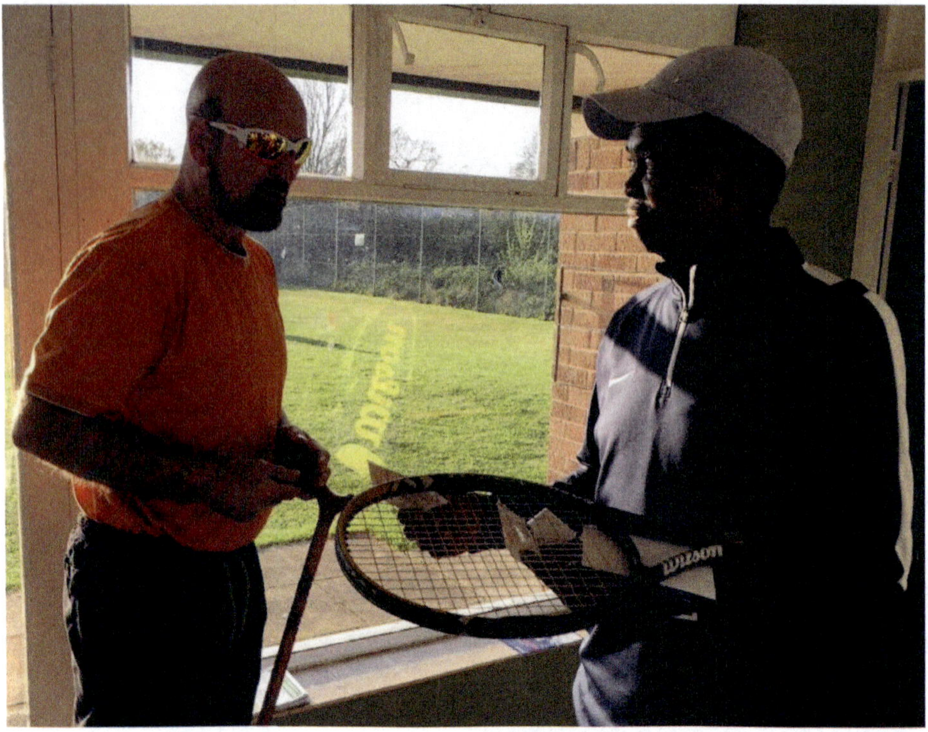
Wilson

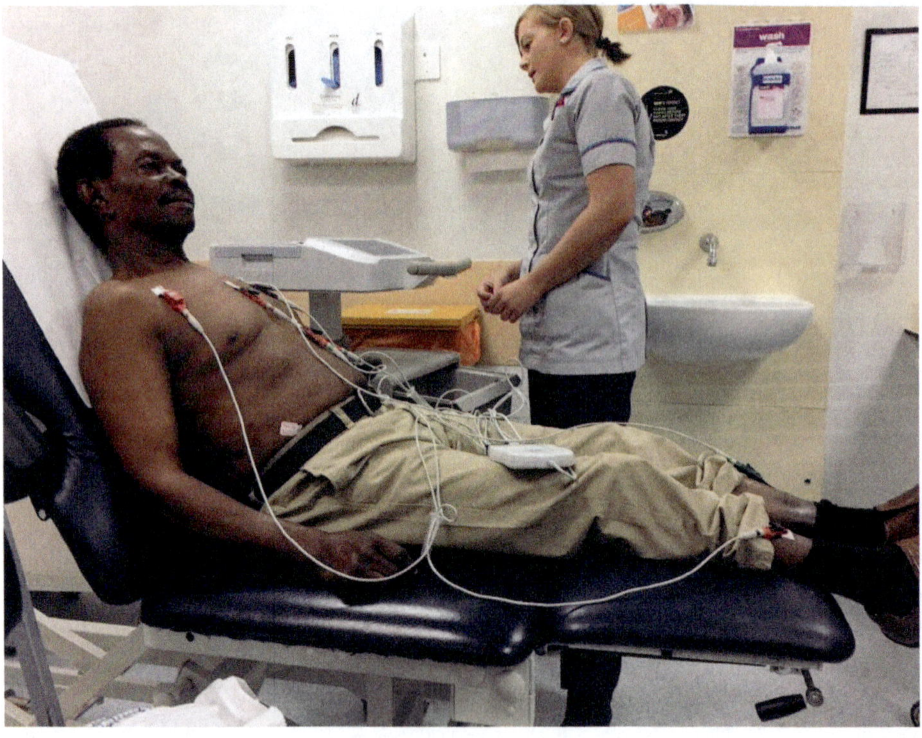
wash

Question 46:

Is it biblical that there is a time for rest? You always say I do too much.

[01/06/2023, 4:01:58 pm] Andrea:

How are you doing

[01/06/2023, 4:03:17 pm] Dad:

I am fine. Just got up to take a mango

[01/06/2023, 4:23:48 pm] Dad:

The Consultant said that I am doing well and will get out of it. It is an aggressive cancer that has to be treated gently because of my age

[01/06/2023, 4:48:51 pm] Andrea:

That is very encouraging

[01/06/2023, 4:49:19 pm] Andrea:

I hope you explained that your grandson is going to the LA Olympics so you need to be there

[01/06/2023, 4:59:59 pm] Dad:

God will perfect everything that concerns us In Jesus Name

[01/06/2023, 5:33:02 pm] Dad:

134/84/94

I will take the drug

[01/06/2023, 7:16:18 pm] Andrea:

Please rest.

[01/06/2023, 7:59:33 pm] Dad:

Just got up for dinner.

[01/06/2023, 10:14:07 pm] Andrea:

Just going to bed. Love you.

[02/06/2023, 7:39:40 am] Dad:

Good morning daughter. Nice talking with you yesterday.

[19/04/2023, 4:10:03 pm] Dad:

Back from the hospital. Tests results were good. Chemo and bone therapy successful also.

Grateful for your prayers

[19/04/2023, 4:27:32 pm] Andrea:

Wow! Well done

[19/04/2023, 4:44:44 pm] Dad:

Next 5 days crucial for after effects. I have all the drugs and water

[19/04/2023, 5:02:42 pm] Andrea:

I've also read that the more chemo you have the more your body gets used to it and sometimes the symptoms can be less.

[19/04/2023, 5:17:07 pm] Dad:

You are right. The side effects are mild now.

Thanks Dr Yetunde Brown

[19/04/2023, 5:18:31 pm] Andrea: 😁

[19/04/2023, 5:20:33 pm] Dad:

You can send me your consultation bill in Naira o

[19/04/2023, 5:21:03 pm] Andrea:

Ha! You would pass out!

Dad:

In Genesis 1 and 2 God created the world in six days and rested on the 7th. It is Biblical.

21st Century King James Version

1 In the beginning God created the heaven and the earth.

2 And the earth was without form and void, and darkness was upon the face of the deep. And the Spirit of God moved upon the face of the waters.

3 And God said, "Let there be light"; and there was light.

4 And God saw the light, that it was good; and God divided the light from the darkness.

5 And God called the light Day, and the darkness He called Night. And the evening and the morning were the first day.

6 And God said, "Let there be a firmament in the midst of the waters, and let it divide the waters from the waters."

7 And God made the firmament, and divided the waters which were under the firmament from the waters which were above the firmament; and it was so.

8 And God called the firmament Heaven. And the evening and the morning were the second day.

9 And God said, "Let the waters under the heaven be gathered together unto one place, and let the dry land appear"; and it was so.

10 And God called the dry land Earth; and the gathering together of the waters called He Seas; and God saw that it was good.

11 And God said, "Let the earth bring forth grass, the herb yielding seed, and the fruit tree yielding fruit after his kind, whose seed is in itself, upon the earth"; and it was so.

12 And the earth brought forth grass, and herb yielding seed after his kind, and the tree yielding fruit, whose seed was in itself, after his kind; and God saw that it was good.

13 And the evening and the morning were the third day.

14 And God said, "Let there be lights in the firmament of the heaven to divide the day from the night; and let them be for signs and for seasons, and for days and years;

15 and let them be for lights in the firmament of the heaven to give light upon the earth"; and it was so.

16 And God made two great lights: the greater light to rule the day, and the lesser light to rule the night. He made the stars also.

17 And God set them in the firmament of the heaven to give light upon the earth,

18 and to rule over the day and over the night, and to divide the light from the darkness. And God saw that it was good.

19 And the evening and the morning were the fourth day.

20 And God said, "Let the waters bring forth abundantly the moving creature that hath life, and fowl that may fly above the earth in the open firmament of heaven."

21 And God created great whales and every living creature that moveth, which the waters brought forth abundantly after their kind, and every winged fowl after his kind; and God saw that it was good.

22 And God blessed them, saying, "Be fruitful and multiply, and fill the waters in the seas, and let fowl multiply on the earth."

23 And the evening and the morning were the fifth day.

24 And God said, "Let the earth bring forth the living creature after his kind: cattle and creeping thing and beast of the earth after his kind"; and it was so.

25 And God made the beast of the earth after his kind, and cattle after their kind, and every thing that creepeth upon the earth after his kind; and God saw that it was good.

26 And God said, "Let Us make man in Our image, after Our likeness; and let them have dominion over the fish of the sea, and over the fowl of the air, and over the cattle, and over all the earth and over every creeping thing that creepeth upon the earth."

27 So God created man in His own image, in the image of God created He him; male and female created He them.

28 And God blessed them, and God said unto them, "Be fruitful and multiply, and replenish the earth, and subdue it; and have dominion over the fish of the sea, and over the fowl of the air, and over every living thing that moveth upon the earth."

29 And God said, "Behold, I have given you every herb bearing seed which is upon the face of all the earth, and every tree in which is the fruit of a tree yielding seed; to you it shall be for meat.

30 And to every beast of the earth, and to every fowl of the air, and to every

thing that creepeth upon the earth wherein there is life, I have given every green herb for meat"; and it was so.

31 And God saw every thing that He had made, and behold, it was very good. And the evening and the morning were the sixth day.

Genesis 2

21st Century King James Version

2 Thus the heavens and the earth were finished, and all the host of them.

2 And on the seventh day God ended His work which He had made; and He rested on the seventh day from all His work which He had made.

3 And God blessed the seventh day and sanctified it, because in it He had rested from all His work which God created and made.

Genesis 1

New International Version

The Beginning

1 In the beginning God created the heavens and the earth. 2 Now the earth was formless and empty, darkness was over the surface of the deep, and the Spirit of God was hovering over the waters.

3 And God said, "Let there be light," and there was light. 4 God saw that the light was good, and he separated the light from the darkness. 5 God called the light "day," and the darkness he called "night." And there was evening, and there was morning—the first day.

6 And God said, "Let there be a vault between the waters to separate water from water." 7 So God made the vault and separated the water under the vault from the water above it. And it was so. 8 God called the vault "sky." And there was evening, and there was morning—the second day.

9 And God said, "Let the water under the sky be gathered to one place, and let dry ground appear." And it was so. 10 God called the dry ground "land," and the gathered waters he called "seas." And God saw that it was good.

11 Then God said, "Let the land produce vegetation: seed-bearing plants and trees on the land that bear fruit with seed in it, according to their various

kinds." And it was so. 12 The land produced vegetation: plants bearing seed according to their kinds and trees bearing fruit with seed in it according to their kinds. And God saw that it was good. 13 And there was evening, and there was morning—the third day.

14 And God said, "Let there be lights in the vault of the sky to separate the day from the night, and let them serve as signs to mark sacred times, and days and years, 15 and let them be lights in the vault of the sky to give light on the earth." And it was so. 16 God made two great lights—the greater light to govern the day and the lesser light to govern the night. He also made the stars. 17 God set them in the vault of the sky to give light on the earth, 18 to govern the day and the night, and to separate light from darkness. And God saw that it was good. 19 And there was evening, and there was morning—the fourth day.

20 And God said, "Let the water teem with living creatures, and let birds fly above the earth across the vault of the sky." 21 So God created the great creatures of the sea and every living thing with which the water teems and that moves about in it, according to their kinds, and every winged bird according to its kind. And God saw that it was good. 22 God blessed them and said, "Be fruitful and increase in number and fill the water in the seas, and let the birds increase on the earth." 23 And there was evening, and there was morning—the fifth day.

24 And God said, "Let the land produce living creatures according to their kinds: the livestock, the creatures that move along the ground, and the wild animals, each according to its kind." And it was so. 25 God made the wild animals according to their kinds, the livestock according to their kinds, and all the creatures that move along the ground according to their kinds. And God saw that it was good.

26 Then God said, "Let us make mankind in our image, in our likeness, so that they may rule over the fish in the sea and the birds in the sky, over the livestock and all the wild animals,[a] and over all the creatures that move along the ground."

27 So God created mankind in his own image,
    in the image of God he created them;
    male and female he created them.

28 God blessed them and said to them, "Be fruitful and increase in number; fill the earth and subdue it. Rule over the fish in the sea and the birds in the sky and over every living creature that moves on the ground."

29 Then God said, "I give you every seed-bearing plant on the face of the whole earth and every tree that has fruit with seed in it. They will be yours for

food. 30 And to all the beasts of the earth and all the birds in the sky and all the creatures that move along the ground—everything that has the breath of life in it—I give every green plant for food." And it was so.

31 God saw all that he had made, and it was very good. And there was evening, and there was morning—the sixth day.

 Genesis 2

New International Version

2 Thus the heavens and the earth were completed in all their vast array.

2 By the seventh day God had finished the work he had been doing; so on the seventh day he rested from all his work. 3 Then God blessed the seventh day and made it holy, because on it he rested from all the work of creating that he had done.

Question 47:

Job's life looked like a disaster because he lost everything. However in Job 42 v 12 his latter end was a blessing.

[20/04/2023, 9:50:02 am] Dad:

Good morning daughter

It was great speaking with you yesterday

Jack's ordeal was a divine plan to provide him a platform to excel in life. It is also a call for the family to draw closer to our Maker.

God has made an utter end and affliction will not arise the 2nd time In Jesus Name

Please tell my grandchildren not to hide much from you in order to receive 1st hand counsel and instructions

Please have a great day and stay safe

[20/04/2023, 11:47:53 am] Andrea:

Hi Dad

It was wonderful chatting to you too. I also should have shared with you sooner to receive my own counsel!

[21/04/2023, 7:49:32 pm] Dad:

God will use anyone to achieve His purpose.

[23/04/2023, 9:10:35 am] Dad:

Good morning daughter. A bit clumsy but I am ready for Church.

[23/04/2023, 2:33:45 pm] Andrea:

Hi Dad

[23/04/2023, 2:33:57 pm] Andrea:

I'm here at Regionals in Somerset with India

[23/04/2023, 3:30:18 pm] Dad:

Congratulations. Happy swimming

[23/04/2023, 4:10:07 pm] Dad:

May God grant you journey mercy back to Bristol. About 1 hour?

[23/04/2023, 4:28:50 pm] Andrea:

Yes about one hour. Long weekend!

[23/04/2023, 4:29:00 pm] Andrea:

Thank you Daddy-O!

[23/04/2023, 4:35:01 pm] Dad:

You are always on my mind

[23/04/2023, 5:03:01 pm] Andrea:

And you are always on mine. 🥰

[23/04/2023, 5:03:43 pm] Andrea:

Last race of the weekend and a bronze medal with a huge time improvement!

[23/04/2023, 5:20:25 pm] Dad:

It is The Lord's doing

[23/04/2023, 5:20:36 pm] Andrea:

Absolutely

[25/04/2023, 2:20:15 pm] Andrea:

Do you know I have a journal all about my relationship with you!

[25/04/2023, 2:20:26 pm] Andrea:

I started it in 2002

[25/04/2023, 2:20:55 pm] Andrea:

I found all sorts in there that I forgot about

[25/04/2023, 2:21:14 pm] Andrea:

I forgot about the days before WhatsApp when we used to write and then email so much.

[25/04/2023, 2:22:12 pm] Andrea:

… and finally I found your handwritten story!

[25/04/2023, 2:22:52 pm] Andrea:

I have it all here so I can type that up.

[25/04/2023, 2:26:56 pm] Dad:

I never knew. I will read this when my head is clearer. But I am not surprised.

[26/04/2023, 11:13:14 am] Andrea:

I chased two consultancy opportunities this week. Disappointing that I didn't get the final agreements this week but both still sound positive

 Job 42:12

21st Century King James Version

12 So the Lord blessed the latter end of Job more than his beginning; for he had fourteen thousand sheep, and six thousand camels, and a thousand yoke of oxen, and a thousand sheasses.

 Job 42:12

New International Version

12 The Lord blessed the latter part of Job's life more than the former part. He had fourteen thousand sheep, six thousand camels, a thousand yoke of oxen and a thousand donkeys.

Question 48:

Can I have a prayer for money worries please Dad.

[26/04/2023, 11:46:35 am] Dad:

As you are striving, you will be achieving by God's grace

[26/04/2023, 11:52:51 am] Dad:

Just a bit concerned about your expenses. I know that you will not lack.

I wish I had some money to send to you. I am only living on passive income but I am fine

[26/04/2023, 12:49:25 pm] Andrea:

I am absolutely fine for now.

[26/04/2023, 12:49:43 pm] Andrea:

Don't worry. Even if you had money I wouldn't take it.

[26/04/2023, 1:11:28 pm] Dad:

Remember the words of the Lord Jesus, that He Himself said, 'It is more blessed to give than to receive'" (**Acts 20:35**). Above all else, giving draws our heart to Christ.1 Oct 2021

 Acts 20:35

21st Century King James Version

35 I have shown you all things, how that by so laboring ye ought to support the weak and to remember the words of the Lord Jesus, how He said, 'It is more blessed to give than to receive.'"

New International Version

35 In everything I did, I showed you that by this kind of hard work we must help the weak, remembering the words the Lord Jesus himself said: 'It is more blessed to give than to receive.'"

God will bless the trip and grant us good success In Jesus Name

[27/04/2023, 4:24:26 pm] Andrea:

Blessed Assurance!

[27/04/2023, 4:56:40 pm] Dad:

One of my favorite songs. Thanks for sharing

[27/04/2023, 5:00:31 pm] Dad:

I testify that The Lord is good all the time

[27/04/2023, 5:04:35 pm] Andrea:

and all the time The Lord is good!

[27/04/2023, 5:04:39 pm] Andrea:

Amen

[27/04/2023, 5:05:06 pm] Andrea:

I like this version. I just heard it on the radio for the first time today. It's by David Leonard Cain.

[27/04/2023, 5:07:03 pm] Dad:

I never heard it like this before.

The other one is Amazing Grace.

[27/04/2023, 6:05:34 pm] Andrea:

Yes. I like that too, but it always reminds me of funerals.

[27/04/2023, 6:05:43 pm] Andrea:

Tyres checked and all good.

[27/04/2023, 6:32:06 pm] Dad:

Please rest well. Just back from my walk

[27/04/2023, 7:02:14 pm] Dad:

We have not had electricity for 4 days. It went off during a heavy rain. Our generator is overwhelmed. We are fine

[27/04/2023, 7:11:59 pm] Dad:

I am sat outside enjoying the breeze. Not too dark yet but hot inside

[27/04/2023, 8:00:28 pm] Andrea:

How lovely

[27/04/2023, 8:00:34 pm] Andrea:

What's the temperature?

[27/04/2023, 9:18:43 pm] Dad:

25 degrees, C

[28/04/2023, 6:47:25 am] Dad:

Good morning all

As you drive to Plymouth today, God will go with you, abide with you and give you all round success In Jesus Name. You will return to Bristol in joy

[28/04/2023, 6:48:00 am] Andrea:

Thank you so much Dad. We are just leaving for morning swimming.

Amazing Grace

By John Newton.

John Newton was an English evangelical Anglican cleric and slavery abolitionist. He had previously been a captain of slave ships and an investor in the slave trade. He served as a sailor in the Royal Navy and was himself enslaved for a time in West Africa.

Amazing grace how sweet the sound

That saved a wretch like me

I once was lost, but now I'm found

Was blind but now I see

'Twas grace that taught my heart to fear

And grace my fears relieved

How precious did that grace appear

The hour I first believed

Through many dangers, toils, and snares

I have already come

This grace that brought me safe thus far

And grace will lead me home

When we've been here ten thousand years

Bright, shining as the sun

We've no less days to sing God's praise

Than when we first begun

Amazing grace how sweet the sound

That saved a wretch like me

I once was lost, but now I'm found

Was blind but now I see

[28/04/2023, 8:18:42 pm] Dad:

Good evening family

How is the swimming progressing

[28/04/2023, 9:23:08 pm] Andrea:

Hi Daddy. We are all fine. Tired but it is going well. Thanks for checking in on us. I love you.

Question 49:

I'm on a diet..again! Do you think it's biblical to look after our bodies?

Dad:

Yes. The bible says so.

[29/04/2023, 11:59:24 am] Dad:

I was a 100 meter runner in school

[29/04/2023, 12:01:27 pm] Andrea:

I never knew that.

[29/04/2023, 12:01:38 pm] Andrea:

I'm sure that helped your tennis.

[29/04/2023, 12:07:14 pm] Dad:

It did and football also I trained in Blackburn but I had to withdraw when I had a Saturday job. All I had from playing was the outfit and transport. I needed to survive. The coach loved my speed.

[29/04/2023, 12:08:12 pm] Andrea:

Your investment in your fitness is paying off now I can promise you!

[29/04/2023, 12:08:32 pm] Andrea:

Please try and do some light weights for your bones and strength

[29/04/2023, 12:08:42 pm] Andrea:

Even with tins of tomatoes!

[29/04/2023, 12:10:32 pm] Dad:

With tins of tomatoes? How?

1 Corinthians 3:16-17

21st Century King James Version

16 Know ye not that ye are the temple of God, and that the Spirit of God dwelleth in you?

17 If any man defile the temple of God, him shall God destroy. For the temple of God is holy, and ye are that temple.

1 Corinthians 3:16-17

New International Version

16 Don't you know that you yourselves are God's temple and that God's Spirit dwells in your midst? 17 If anyone destroys God's temple, God will destroy that person; for God's temple is sacred, and you together are that temple.

1 Corinthians 6:19-20

21st Century King James Version

19 What? Know ye not that your body is the temple of the Holy Ghost which is in you and which ye have from God, and that ye are not your own?

20 For ye are bought with a price. Therefore glorify God in your body and in your spirit, which are God's.

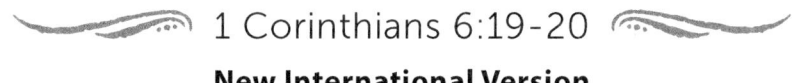

1 Corinthians 6:19-20

New International Version

19 Do you not know that your bodies are temples of the Holy Spirit, who is in you, whom you have received from God? You are not your own; 20 you were bought at a price. Therefore honor God with your bodies.

Question 50:

Can you share some of your miracles?

Prayers for debt owed to us to be repaid, bringing just in time financial help

[29/04/2023, 12:25:23 pm] Dad:

A Tennant packed out of the house 2015 March without paying. He left a promissory note to pay in 3 months. He never did and I stopped asking him. I still send him daily scripture.

2022 he paid part.

Just now he asked for the balance and paid up. Here's what he wrote:

[29/04/2023, 12:26:10 pm] Dad:

Good morning sir. I trust you're keeping well. Could you kindly let me know how much I have to settle and if the First bank account remains your preference for payment?

Many thanks sir

[29/04/2023, 12:26:11 pm] Dad:

Good morning Mr Tayo. It is only 30k

Bola Ogunkoya and yes that is my bank.

Thanks

[29/04/2023, 12:26:11 pm] Dad:

ALAT Transfer Receipt ₦30,000.00 - Saturday, April 29,

[29/04/2023, 12:26:12 pm] Dad:

From him: Payment made sir. Apologies for the inconveniences.

[29/04/2023, 12:26:12 pm] Dad:

Thanks

[29/04/2023, 12:26:45 pm] Andrea:

Amazing!

[29/04/2023, 12:26:51 pm] Dad:

God is good

[29/04/2023, 12:27:31 pm] Andrea:

SO, SO good!

[29/04/2023, 12:30:26 pm] Dad:

That company will surely settle your outstanding amount.

Prayers to slow down answered.

Andrea launched a major non profit initiative producing a documentary on mental health for athletes.

[01/05/2023, 9:03:12 am] Dad:

Good morning daughter. No school today?

[01/05/2023, 9:07:45 am] Andrea:

It's a bank holiday

[01/05/2023, 9:08:11 am] Andrea:

Also the teachers are on strike so no school tomorrow but lots of exam revision

[01/05/2023, 9:09:34 am] Andrea:

You would not believe how many people know me at these swimming events! Loads from all over coming up to me and chatting.

[01/05/2023, 9:17:50 am] Dad:

Today is Workers day and a holiday

You have been in the swimming industry for a long time.

I'm surprised that you have not been given a National Award

You at least have my award!

[01/05/2023, 9:19:37 am] Andrea:

Awww Dad. That made me smile SO much.

[01/05/2023, 9:26:52 am] Dad:

Your steadfastness and perseverance gladden my heart and make me proud.

[01/05/2023, 9:28:02 am] Andrea:

Thank you Dad. ❤️ I learned from a 78 year old man I know.

[01/05/2023, 9:38:21 am] Dad:

My prayer is that in the next 10 years you would have been done with very active activities and retired to enjoy your life.

[01/05/2023, 9:40:17 am] Andrea:

I will slow down but never stop! I love it and my grandchildren will be involved in competitive sport of some sort I'm sure. I would like to have the financial freedom to do more charity work.

[01/05/2023, 9:51:22 am] Dad:

Amen.

Prayers of protection answered. Limited injury and healed quickly.

[05/05/2023, 6:01:13 am] Dad:

Good morning daughter. Please join me in thanking God

I went to the bathroom 2am without my usual small flash light

I came out and instead of reaching for the bed I went on the floor. I shouted. Niyi was on hand to my rescue. I didn't hit my head on the tiles just my knees and hand. Painful but I thank God

[05/05/2023, 6:01:47 am] Andrea:

Oh my goodness!

[05/05/2023, 6:02:23 am] Andrea:

Thank you Jesus.

[05/05/2023, 6:03:07 am] Andrea:

Not only the physical but the shock could have killed you. We thank God.

[05/05/2023, 6:19:56 am] Dad:

A few we know passed on this way

Niyi treated me and I feel OK but my right hand

I used the hands to protect my head when I was falling

We have a hospital appointment today but I may shift it to Monday

[05/05/2023, 6:51:23 am] Andrea:

That's good reflex still!

[05/05/2023, 7:30:55 am] Dad:

You are right about the shock. When Niyi helped me up I sat on the floor for a while to regain my balance

[05/05/2023, 7:31:57 am] Andrea:

You may have a sprained or even fractured wrist. How does it feel?

[05/05/2023, 9:53:41 am] Dad:

Just painful. Some other pains are just manifesting. I will be alright. Thanks

[05/05/2023, 10:01:21 am] Andrea:

Yes and probably even more sore tomorrow. That's enough excitement for the day!

[05/05/2023, 10:02:13 am] Andrea:

Get some ice on the areas that hurt and try and elevate your hands a bit like resting them on your chest when you are sitting up.

[05/05/2023, 10:02:37 am] Andrea:

Dr. Andrea Yetunde here again! 😁

Prayers for good exam results answered - 1500 in SAT

[06/05/2023, 6:04:23 am] Andrea:

Thanks Dad. This morning is another exam in Somerset. It's a lot for him and he's tired so I need to make sure I'm looking after him mentally. Very challenging time.

[06/05/2023, 6:12:19 am] Dad:

Mind set. Determination. Experience. He will. He can

Blessedness!

[06/05/2023, 6:40:42 am] Dad:

In psalm 126 v 5 that he who sows in tears will come back home rejoicing

Jack is sowing now with lots of difficulties but only for a while

The seeds will germinate and bring us all a bountiful harvest!

[06/05/2023, 7:46:03 am] Andrea:

Amen to that!

[06/05/2023, 7:46:42 am] Andrea:

He's just gone in. It starts at 8am. I'm going to find somewhere for a hot drink.

[06/05/2023, 8:10:33 am] Dad:

God will watch over you both for good In Jesus Name

 Philippians 4:4-6

21st Century King James Version

4 Rejoice in the Lord always; and again I say, "Rejoice!"

5 Let your moderation be known to all men. The Lord is at hand.

6 Fret not about anything, but in everything, by prayer and supplication with thanksgiving, let your requests be made known unto God.

Read Philippians 4 v 4-6 again and Rejoice!

 Philippians 4:4-6

New International Version

Final Exhortations

4 Rejoice in the Lord always. I will say it again: Rejoice! 5 Let your gentleness be evident to all. The Lord is near. 6 Do not be anxious about anything, but in every situation, by prayer and petition, with thanksgiving, present your requests to God.

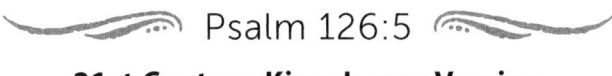 Psalm 126:5

21st Century King James Version

5 They that sow in tears shall reap in joy.

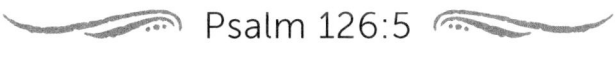 Psalm 126:5

New International Version

5 Those who sow with tears

will reap with songs of joy.

I'm trading my sorrows

By Darrell Evans

I'm trading my sorrows

I'm trading my shame

I'm laying them down

For the joy of the Lord

I'm trading my sickness

I'm trading my pain

I'm laying them down

For the joy of the Lord

We say yes Lord yes Lord yes yes Lord

Yes Lord yes Lord yes yes Lord

Yes Lord yes Lord yes yes Lord

Amen

I am pressed but not crushed

Persecuted not abandoned

Struck down but not destroyed

I am blessed beyond the curse

For His promise will endure

That His joy's gonna be my strength

Though the sorrow may last for the night

His joy comes with the morning

We say yes Lord yes Lord yes yes Lord

We say yes Lord yes Lord yes yes Lord

We say yes Lord yes Lord yes yes Lord

Amen

Prayers for money answered.

[09/05/2023, 6:45:13 pm] Andrea:

I've sent you some funds. That's four rounds of treatment and a little extra or whatever you need it for.

[09/05/2023, 6:45:40 pm] Andrea:

The company agreed to my settlement today. I haven't got the money yet but it's coming!

[09/05/2023, 6:46:35 pm] Andrea:

I hope this makes you feel more relaxed and is a nice surprise.

[09/05/2023, 6:49:36 pm] Andrea:

God promises to provide what we need (**Philippians 4:19**, **Matthew 6:31-32**). He created the universe and gives food to every living thing — including you and me. The same God who provides food for the animals will not allow us to go without (**Psalm 145:15-16, Luke 12:24-26**).

 Philippians 4:19

21st Century King James Version

19 But my God shall supply all your need, according to His riches in glory by Christ Jesus.

Philippians 4:19
New International Version

19 And my God will meet all your needs according to the riches of his glory in Christ Jesus.

Matthew 6:31-32
21st Century King James Version

31 Therefore take no thought, saying, 'What shall we eat?' or 'What shall we drink?' or 'Wherewith shall we be clothed?'

32 (For after all these things do the Gentiles seek.) For your heavenly Father knoweth that ye have need of all these things.

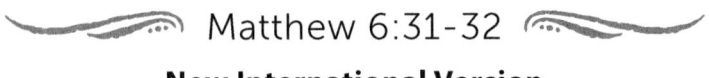
Matthew 6:31-32
New International Version

31 So do not worry, saying, 'What shall we eat?' or 'What shall we drink?' or 'What shall we wear?' 32 For the pagans run after all these things, and your heavenly Father knows that you need them.

Psalm 145:15-16
21st Century King James Version

15 The eyes of all wait upon Thee, and Thou givest them their meat in due season.

16 Thou openest Thine hand, and satisfiest the desire of every living thing.

21st Century King James Version

15 The eyes of all wait upon Thee, and Thou givest them their meat in due season.

16 Thou openest Thine hand, and satisfiest the desire of every living thing.

[09/05/2023, 7:14:26 pm] Dad:

Good evening daughter. It is a nice surprise. I can only say a big thank you. We are grateful to God for His mercy and provision.

Resting again tomorrow for Thursday tests and the procedure on Friday

God bless you real good.

[09/05/2023, 7:18:03 pm] Andrea:

How would you feel about including something fun in your program? My thoughts were to either go to a Chinese restaurant with Aunty Niyi or order food in. I know you will see it as perhaps unnecessary and extravagant BUT I think you both deserve something nice. I know the chemo makes you lose your appetite. If you were here I would order you Chinese food! Maybe after your tests tomorrow so Aunty Niyi doesn't have to worry about food?

[09/05/2023, 7:36:54 pm] Dad:

I agree. Thanks. From the hospital on Friday we will have a treat

[09/05/2023, 7:37:11 pm] Andrea:

Can you eat after chemo?

[09/05/2023, 7:40:21 pm] Dad:

Yes. It is recommended. Some weak patients are eating as the Chemo is on to have strength

[09/05/2023, 7:40:35 pm] Andrea:

Wow!

[09/05/2023, 7:41:04 pm] Andrea:

That's a plan then. Let me know where you decide to go.

[09/05/2023, 7:48:55 pm] Dad:

I will. Not before we eat Ha ha. You don't have to pay. Trust that we'll go

There is an interesting football match by 8pm. Man City vs Real Madrid

I hope to watch if we have power else follow the highlights on my phone

[09/05/2023, 8:02:01 pm] Andrea:

Oh that will be great!

[09/05/2023, 9:39:59 pm] Dad:

Thanks, Good night God bless you

[09/05/2023, 10:14:30 pm] Andrea:

Night Dad

[10/05/2023, 5:22:32 am] Andrea:

Good morning Dad!

[10/05/2023, 5:25:15 am] Dad:

Good morning daughter I hope you rested well. Thanks for your magnanimity. God will surely reward you

[10/05/2023, 5:46:26 am] Dad:

God is never late. Just at the time you need help He shows up. At the nick of time.

May His Name be praised forever

[10/05/2023, 6:26:49 am] Dad:

Psalms 46 1

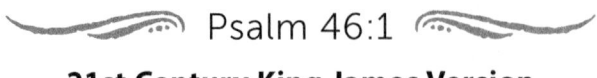

Psalm 46:1

21st Century King James Version

46 God is our refuge and strength, a very present help in trouble.

New International Version

Psalm 46[a]

For the director of music. Of the Sons of Korah. According to alamoth.[b] A song.

1 God is our refuge and strength,

an ever-present help in trouble.

I needed help badly but I dare not ask.

[10/05/2023, 6:41:28 am] Andrea:

That is "God is our refuge and our strength"

[10/05/2023, 6:43:14 am] Andrea:

You don't need to ask. I always know and it's always at the front of my mind. The second I can, I will.

[10/05/2023, 6:43:44 am] Andrea:

Any worship song come to mind?

[10/05/2023, 6:48:22 am] Dad:

In Christ alone

[10/05/2023, 7:06:46 am] Andrea:

Did you watch the football?

[10/05/2023, 7:06:57 am] Andrea:

Draw

[10/05/2023, 7:07:26 am] Andrea:

In this day in history, Nelson Mandela became president

[10/05/2023, 7:41:58 am] Dad:

The issue is this I worry about the fact that you that you are in a rented apartment

I would have been more comfortable in a smaller house called your own. I am sure God will bless you even beyond that In Jesus Name

My TV provider did show the match but other ones. I followed up on my phone. Man City 1 Real Madrid 1.They are the best teams in the world.

Worship Song Recommendation

Who you say I am

By Hillsong

Who am I that the highest King

Would welcome me?

I was lost but He brought me in

Oh His love for me

Oh His love for me

Who the Son sets free

Oh is free indeed

I'm a child of God

Yes I am

Free at last

He has ransomed me

His grace runs deep

While I was a slave to sin

Jesus died for me

Yes, He died for me

Who the Son sets free

Oh is free indeed

I'm a child of God

Yes I am

In my Father's house

There's a place for me

I'm a child of God

Yes I am

I am chosen not forsaken

I am who You say I am

You are for me not against me
I am who You say I am
I am chosen not forsaken
I am who You say I am
You are for me not against me
I am who You say I am
I am who You say I am
Who the Son sets free
Oh is free indeed
I'm a child of God
Yes I am
In my Father's house
There's a place for me
I'm a child of God
Yes I am
In my Father's house
There's a place for me
I'm a child of God
Yes I am

Prayers for sustenance answered.

[11/05/2023, 1:54:19 pm] Andrea:

Hi Dad

[11/05/2023, 1:54:25 pm] Andrea:

How is everything going?

[11/05/2023, 2:34:22 pm] Andrea:

I said you sound SO Good!

[11/05/2023, 2:34:31 pm] Andrea:

10 years younger!

[11/05/2023, 2:34:51 pm] Andrea:

I'm SO thrilled with this news. What a blessing.

[11/05/2023, 2:35:07 pm] Andrea:

God said "not today"!

[11/05/2023, 2:36:31 pm] Dad:

It is a real blessing. Thank you

[11/05/2023, 2:45:04 pm] Dad:

I am careful with money

Today already tested it 6k registration 3k chemo and bone therapy drugs 120k fuel. 5k

So I will see the cost of the Chinese food before I order

[11/05/2023, 2:49:09 pm] Dad:

Yes I just received the debit for the drugs on my phone now 123k

[11/05/2023, 4:37:01 pm] Dad:

OK. We are home now. Thanks

For Chinese I love Corn soup, Spring Rolls, Sweet and sour fish, Shredded chicken, Rice

[11/05/2023, 5:42:38 pm] Andrea:

I am arranging delivery

[11/05/2023, 5:42:49 pm] Andrea:

What time do you want to eat?!

[11/05/2023, 5:43:15 pm] Andrea:

I sent you the menu

[11/05/2023, 5:44:57 pm] Dad:

That is unbelievable! I will ask

[11/05/2023, 5:45:03 pm] Andrea: 😎

[11/05/2023, 5:52:28 pm] Dad:

Who gave you the title for our Book?

[11/05/2023, 5:52:39 pm] Andrea:

I came up with it!

[11/05/2023, 5:52:53 pm] Andrea:

What do you think?

[11/05/2023, 5:53:28 pm] Dad:

That is my girl!

[11/05/2023, 5:53:39 pm] Andrea:

I'm laughing!

[11/05/2023, 5:55:46 pm] Andrea:

Let me know about food when you can because my lovely person at the restaurant is waiting for me. They are wonderful!

[11/05/2023, 6:11:07 pm] Dad:

2.30pm Friday. Niyi, Laide and daddy B. O say a big thank you

[11/05/2023, 6:56:39 pm] Andrea:

Great!

[11/05/2023, 6:56:48 pm] Andrea:

This is my kind of service!

[11/05/2023, 6:57:16 pm] Andrea:

There is hope for Nigeria!

[11/05/2023, 6:59:40 pm] Dad:

I think so. It starts from somewhere!

[11/05/2023, 7:00:17 pm] Dad:

Lovely!

[13/05/2023, 7:48:45 am] Dad:

Good morning daughter How are you all

How is Bisto?

Where is India's Nationals?

I wish you success in everything you do In Jesus Name.

Please remain blessed and pray for me.

[13/05/2023, 8:28:36 am] Andrea:

It's very soon afterwards Dad so just relax into it. Listen to your body. Rest of you need to rest.

[13/05/2023, 8:30:26 am] Dad:

Thanks consultant Y. O

[13/05/2023, 8:30:58 am] Andrea: 😁

[13/05/2023, 8:34:37 am] Dad:

You can notice the confusion from Doctor to Consultant

[13/05/2023, 9:14:13 am] Andrea:

Ha ha I thought I got promoted!

[13/05/2023, 9:23:47 am] Dad:

30 years from Dr. to consultant

[14/05/2023, 5:10:03 am] Dad:

Motherhood is a Test. May we pass.

It is a Responsibility. May we not fail.

It is a Privilege. May we never be ungrateful.

[14/05/2023, 6:45:16 am] Andrea:

Awww… that's lovely Dad. Thank you. How are you doing?

[14/05/2023, 6:48:18 am] Andrea:

Great, GREAT day of swimming with India yesterday. HUGE time improvements, a silver medal in a very difficult race that earned her a place on the national list. It's not guaranteed because if someone swims faster than her she will get bumped off but out of the top 24 she's 18th so her coach thinks she should be safe. She was SO thrilled and proud.

[14/05/2023, 6:52:08 am] Dad:

Congratulations India. Very proud of you. Please keep it up.

Prayers to keep dementia away, answered.

There was a year in my life that I remembered last night. 1957 - 1958

I left the Primary school but found no admission to the secondary school. My dad sent me to a Remedial school in our village Isire. Tough, very tough. But the most instructive part of my life. I will continue from there. You must not miss it.

[25/05/2023, 9:01:20 am] Andrea:

Oh I want to hear more about this!

[25/05/2023, 9:02:48 am] Dad:

You will. God just refreshed my memory last night

[25/05/2023, 9:25:02 am] Andrea:

Beautiful

Prayers of protection, answered.

[25/05/2023, 6:01:19 pm] Dad:

My village Isire is in the North East local government of Ijebu. Ijebu Ode is the main city.

I was sent there by my late father because I couldn't find a secondary school at Ibadan in 1958.

My mother did not like it but there was no argument with my father.

We have a big house in the village. No one lived there but a security man from Kano called Bature.

Bature was a big good natured Hausa man who became my carer for a year.

I did not see my parents or siblings for the period. Bature received a monthly wage from my father but I lived with him. He must have been about 40 with no family.

My Remedial school was about 2 miles away from the village. I walked Monday to Friday

I played football for the school and ran 100 metres and relay.

Bature went hunting for squirrels, rabbits and snails so I joined him 4 pm Friday to 2pm Sunday.

That was our food. No oats. No. Milk. No fruits unless the ones picked up during hunting in the thick forest. No tea. Just water from a stream one mile away.

Daddy had brothers and sisters in the village so I related with them

One woman who was very caring was threshing out Red Palm oil from palm fruits. She would boil the fruits for a long time, drain out the water, put them in jute bags and march on them to squeeze out the palm oil.

She would sell some and give me some for our stew.

The year ended at the Remedial school and I returned to Ibadan where admission had been secured for me at Ibadan Boys High school in 1959.

I never saw Malam Bature again.

Has anyone seen him?

He showed me life. He taught me resistance. He shared his food with me

Please tell me where he's gone!

Andrea:

What an amazing man to look after you like that.

 Galatians 6:9

New Living Translation
(Dad prefers this translation for this scripture.)

9 So let's not get tired of doing what is good. At just the right time we will reap a harvest of blessing if we don't give up.

 Galatians 6:9

21st Century King James Version

9 And let us not be weary in welldoing, for in due season we shall reap, if we faint not.

 Galatians 6:9

New International Version

9 Let us not become weary in doing good, for at the proper time we will reap a harvest if we do not give up.

Dad April 27th 2023:

My heart's desire is that this scriptural knowledge is passed on to my grandchildren. We recite psalms 23 and 91 in this house daily. Will they grow up and ask you some of the questions you are asking me?

Legacy!

Andrea:

Ha! I promise you with all my heart that every single thing you have told me will be passed down to them and their children. When they ask questions I will quickly grab our book and quote from it sounding wise!

Writing this book is the most I have read the bible in my whole life!

Dad:

Just God!

Luke 12:24-26

21st Century King James Version

24 Consider the ravens: for they neither sow nor reap, they neither have storehouse nor barn, and God feedeth them. How much more are ye better than the fowls?

25 And which of you by taking thought can add to his stature one cubit?

26 If ye then be not able to do that thing which is least, why take ye thought for the rest?

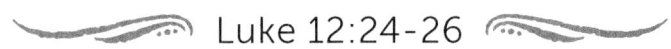

Luke 12:24-26

New International Version

24 Consider the ravens: They do not sow or reap, they have no storeroom or barn; yet God feeds them. And how much more valuable you are than birds!

25 Who of you by worrying can add a single hour to your life[a]? 26 Since you cannot do this very little thing, why do you worry about the rest?

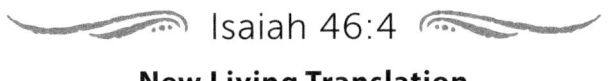

Isaiah 46:4

New Living Translation

New Living Translation

I will be your God throughout your lifetime —

until your hair is white with age.

I made you, and I will care for you.

I will carry you along and save you.

Index of Bible Verses

Index of Worship songs

13/6/2023

Andrea:

I will really miss you when you're gone Dad

Dad:

We would meet again

Andrea:

In Jesus Mighty Name

Dad:

Amen

Printed in Great Britain
by Amazon

25131147R00139